The Energy and Science

of

Crown ReiQi

I0161477

The History Behind Its Origin

by

Rene Qian

Copyright© 2022 Rene Qian
All rights reserved
Photography: Natalia Antarez Ramirez
Artwork and Cover Design, by Rene Qian
Phoenix, AZ

First Edition 2022©
Rene Qian

Book Title:
Energy and Science of Crown ReiQi©-The History Behind Its Origin
ISBN 978-1-7354096-6-5 (paperback).

PUBLISHER'S NOTE

The *Crown ReiQi©* modality was created based on the principles of the Traditional Usui Reiki System empowered by the Usui Reiki symbols; three mantras derived from these symbols, and the pristine symbol of the *Crown ReiQi©* modality.

Without limiting the rights under copyright reserved above, no part of this publication may be reproduced, stored in, or introduced into a retrieval system or transmitted, in any form or by any means (electronic, mechanical, photocopying, recording or otherwise), existing or non-existing, known, or unknown, without the prior written permission of both the copyright owner and the above publisher of this book.

The scanning, uploading, and distribution of the book via Internet or via any other means without the permission of the publisher is illegal and punishable by law. Please purchase only authorized electronic editions, and do not participate in or encourage electronic piracy of copyrighted materials. Your support of the author's right is appreciated.

DISCLAIMER

This intellectual work was created to provide information and techniques that have been practiced for many years around the world. Such information and practices apply a set of systems within the human body; nevertheless, no claims have been filed regarding its effectiveness.

Medical advice is encouraged before engaging in such endeavors.

The author and publisher of this publication are not responsible in any way for any harm that may occur through following the instructions in this book.

This energetic modality during the exercise process holds the emotional and spiritual satisfaction of the practitioner with results based on individual perception. This knowledge is based on the author's own experience and on the practice of the teachings of qualified masters in the spiritual arts.

There is no promise that a terminal illness can be catalyzed by practicing this modality, but it is recommended that you consult your primary physician before embarking on this knowledge.

DISCLAIMER

TABLE OF CONTENTS

Prologue 1

Introduction 5

Chapter One 9
  The First Contact.. 9

Chapter Two...13
  Broken Brains 13
    Reasons why a stroke may happen.................................. 14
    The need to observe the scientific method 15

Chapter Three...19
  Reiki Rules to Keep Growth and Discipline 19
    Sunrise after Confusion.. 21
    Direct Bearer of the Usui Healing System 22
    Phyllis Furumoto, Bearer of a Bifurcated Energy Realm........... 22
    Rippled Action Effects 23
    Universal Life Force for All.. 24
    Reiki before Mikao Usui 28

Chapter Four 33
  Recreating Dr. Mikao Usui's Reiki...................................... 33
    Seekers Finding Their Own Way 33
    Reiki Modalities 35
    Healing the Physical Body First, the Rest will Follow............... 37
    Reiki's benefits: 37
    Energy Medicine's Setback Development 40
    A Twisted Hop Within the Medical Area........................ 49

Chapter Five..51
  Science Vs. Vital Energy 51
    What happened here? 51

Anesthesia's Toxicity 52

Hematologic Manifestations 54

Allergic Manifestations 55

There are three types of chemical ligands: 60

Reiki Scope Goes Beyond All Paradigms 61

The Tangling of Energy Fields 67

Discharge of other Vital Energy Modalities 69

The *Crown ReiQi*© Master Modality 71

Chapter Six 73

The History Behind Its Origin 73

The Order of the Factors Does Not Alter the Product 73

The History Behind Its Origin 79

Incidents Vibrate within the Superstrings 82

The Crystal Skulls 85

Honoring Skull Celebration 86

Sacredness of the Human Body 89

Notes 91

Prologue 91

Introduction 91

Chapter One 92

Chapter Two 92

Chapter Three 92

Chapter Four 93

Chapter Five 96

Chapter Six 97

Bibliography 99

PROLOGUE

Dr. Mikao Usui, gave the best gift mankind would deserve. Spiritual history tells us about a priest who went to the desert for 21 days and then through the process of a heavenly blessing he finds out he had met the crossroad of energy fields he called Reiki.[1]

There is not a direct account of the works of Mikao Usui, which this would be the original and only Reiki, but instead we have the message perceived from Mikao Usui through one of his disciples or followers, Hayashi, which in turn taught Takata.[2]

Their predisposition to share such perceived panacea opened a Pandora' box for all its followers.

There are other versions besides the one Hayashi shared to Takata. Remember that Usui had other disciples and as well these spread their perception of what Usui's teachings were.

Hayashi taught his disciples according of what he had perceived from Usui's teachings. Takata as well, taught her disciples according to what she had perceived from Hayashi's teachings.

Later in 1998, for the first time outside of Japan, was published a revealing book, showing Dr. Mikao Usui's hand positions about this healing system.[3]

During Phyllis Lei Furumoto's performance as the direct lineage holder of the Usui system in the West, many students demanded to be granted with the attunements of the 3rd Usui System Reiki Level, so them could attune other interested students on the transmission of the Energy Life Force. The pressure increased to alarming levels within Usui's headquarters to the point where many of the students began to deny Phyllis' authority, achieving finally the rupture of the institution of the Usui system. The lineage transmitted to Phyllis Lei Furumoto by the Grand Master of the Usui system Hawayo Takata, grandmother of Phyllis Lei Furumoto, was divided.

Time went by before practitioners from the 1st and 2nd Usui system Reiki degree could receive the Third Level Reiki attunement.

Through Phyllis, other students who after had received the attunements, became masters and third level practitioners. The lineage spread to other schools disguising with different expressions the true Usui's teachings, but not its essence.

From these ramifications at this point, there can be numbered many other Reiki modalities, around one hundred.

As far as I'm concerned, there's nothing by Usui's own handwriting, from the beginning of his teachings.[4] His followers -according to the western tradition- like Hayashi and Takata have interpreted Usui's teachings. Inscription of the Usui's system may be found in a memorial stone from a public cemetery in Tokyo.

Spiritual insights are an intimate experience so, Reiki leaders share their insights about these experiences making them public as a set of principles or rules to be followed by the adepts. From this stand, it seems Usui's teachings left an open gate for other Universal force's manifestations, still being pursued for all Reiki practitioners around the world.

Like many other Energy practitioners who have discovered and written their own modality, I came up with the *Crown ReiQi©* modality. Based on the principle that every human being is a spark from this enormous and vast universe, and if new neophyte practice thoroughly searching for the purest, I'm sure there will be many other Reiki modalities to come.

INTRODUCTION

Clinical scientists have discovered that all our thoughts, dreams, experiences, and memories are kept in the neural networks in the brain, even traumas, addictions, lack of confidence and so forth, might develop a self-negative belief system which are also stored in certain areas of the brain.

The Energy and Science of Crown ReiQi© and The History Behind its Origin, is about how the scientific and the spiritual domain meet, and after comparing their principles, both end as a reflection of one another when trying to explain its semantic fields, when applied to the scientific method. Both the scientific guild and the spiritual conduits agree that the crystallization of their beliefs must comply with the laws of matter, which in turn, must be subdued by the intangible fields of electromagnetism derived from the nature of the atomic presence.

The theme of the beginnings of the *Crown ReiQi©* modality is also explored, as the beginning and background of the central figure of this modality: the crystal skull.

The definition of matter is a material substance that constitutes the observable cosmos which together with energy, forms the basis of all objective phenomena. In the case when referring to vital or universal energy, it is composed by atoms which are the essence of the mystery of energy. Let's agree the Universe is formed by energy and based on this principle, spiritual modalities relate to the power of the energies from the universe, connecting life as a way of a sacred gift provided by nature since birth.

Since the earliest civilizations, humans have developed their forms of communication not only through the power of speech, but also through drawings and markings, which are now found in caves and in the natural landscape. Rituals involved the participation of specialized groups in the invocation of elementals as a means of interpreting the manifestation of the gods.

The work of energetic and spiritual knowledge was a common practice century ago, long before religions were stablished as institutions. Humankind related to their reality according to the spiritual forces of nature and domestic customs. Sages, shamans, witchcraft, and oracles were the rule to live in harmony in every social circle. Papyrus was first used to pass magic spells and effective prayers to reach the magical forces. Later, books were written to preserve this mystical and sacred knowledge. Nowadays mouth to mouth knowledge is still practiced keeping the power and strength of the unmanifested forces but released when uttered.

Practicing *Crown ReiQi*© or Chi-kung involves the regulation of breathing, which translates as an exchange of gases in which oxygen to carbon dioxide is involved through the breathing process, to preserve life. Focusing your attention on the breathing cycles will provide within the practitioner a living force which is connected to the "spirit" within the air in the environment. This air according to energy work practitioners, contains an etheric fluid which may be projected by intention as an electro-magnetic field through certain body part movements; even breath, sight and mind may manipulate such electro-magnetic field.

This though is far-off to be part of the scientific guild knowledge which philosophy is based particularly on the scientific method.[1]

Scientists have brought to life the concept of new parameters to measure the brain activity such as *Functional Magnetic Resonance Imaging* (fMRI), to detect the presence of the blood's oxygen in the brain; the *Diffusion Tensor Imaging* (DTI), which detects the brain's water flow; the Electro Encephalogram (EEG), which explores the depths of the brain; the *Positron Emission Tomography* (PET), which calculates the brain's energy flow tracking down glucose presence, the sugar's molecule, and the cell's fluid. Other scientific tools are the *Transcranial Electromagnetic Scanner* (TES), the *Magneto Encephalo Graph* (MEG), the *Near-InfraRed Spectroscopy* (NIRS), the *Deep Brain Stimulation* (DBS), other outstanding scientific discovery has been *Optogenetics,* most commonly refers to a biological technique that involves the use of light to control cells in living tissue, typically neurons, that have been genetically modified to express light-sensitive ion channels,[2] and the *Clarity,* which is a method of making brain tissue transparent, which key point is to eliminate the cell's lipids -that tend to provide an opaque look to the brain- keeping neurons intact.[3]

The scientific guild and energy workers have built their knowledge foundation on several grounds, and although there are differences on their practice and on their ways to explain their results, both ways will at the long run serve patients and energy recipients. One side has built its reality upon physical results, its counterpart has seen results based on spiritual precepts, but both have followed and pursued the discipline to gain knowledge. Education is experience, which context and information after exposure and delivery, by an accredited associated with a degree will be accepted by the regimen of disciplines and ideas. This principle must be followed by dogmatic thinkers and medical scientists to be validated by stablished magisterial institutions.

Energy workers as well as the scientific guild, have been working on their areas to share proof of validation about their beliefs and practices. There will be always two opposing groups, even belonging to the spiritual realm, who will try to express their points of view as true. Even inside the scientific realm, there will be more than one group which will support and defend their points of view as the latest discovery, to have proof of cure of the worst disease in the neighborhood.

The scientific latest discoveries must be supported by the knowledge of their predecessors to own validity, these must be probed according to the scientific method and the approval of the medical association which acknowledged them. Same principle applies to the subtle energy associations, knowledge must be bestowed by an experienced teacher to their students or neophytes. Instructors need to show authenticity of their practices with satisfactory results on every spiritual intervention.

Recognized scientific figures as well as spiritual leaders and practices must be exposed to thorough examination, so its mission and purpose be considered in the elements and logic of discoveries and anomalies and the structure of discoveries,[4] so latter, after scrutiny may appear on official reports of scientific and educational institutions.

Aggressive illnesses such as Alzheimer's and other dementias; Parkinson's; cirrhosis; tuberculosis; dehydration due to diarrheal diseases; diabetes mellitus; trachea, bronchus, and lung cancers; chronic obstructive pulmonary disease; lower respiratory infections; stroke, ischemic heart disease or coronary artery disease,[5] are being treated by the medical institutions, but energy work practitioners are wondering about its correlation with the emotional and low energy levels which might be important factors for these illnesses to ravage humanity.

Fights against disease belong to the medical profession, but the practice of energy work belongs to seekers of dark forces within the mind such as stress, lack of attachment from childhood and traumatic experiences, backed with the intention factor, to improve the flow of energy around the body so that practitioners can enable relaxation, reduce pain, accelerate the healing process, harmful emotional experiences and reduce other symptoms of mental, psychological and nuclear physical illnesses.[6]

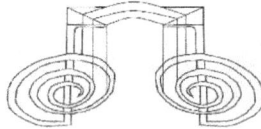

CHAPTER ONE

THE FIRST CONTACT

In 1998 I was introduced to the magic of Reiki, and the memory is still fresh in my mind that few people knew about this system of energy transmission. When I talked to people in El Paso, Texas, about this energetic modality, they would just look at me with a blank stare, oblivious to what I was trying to tell them, or about Transcendental Meditation-TM, Chi kung or another energetic modality, most of my peers were culturally uninformed about such invisible and cosmic influences.

El Paso, in 2005, was in an expansion project, but not to the expansion of ideas, but to the financial trends that were flourishing at that time in the region.

Now in 2019, Reiki has been linked to the source of flourishment. On every soul who has learned the basic hand Usui's Reiki positions, there also has been implanted a seed with unimaginable outburst results.

Concerned practitioners don't tend to treat physical ailments, for this is an area where the medical field has been working for centuries, and from the ethical and professional point of view, people with a chronic physical pain rather go first to their family physician. Reiki practitioners are aware of these legal implications, so they provide their services on the principle that universal energy pursues balance when in touch with someone in need.

Physical ailments are the outcome of a long process from an environment exposure.

Social, financial, culture, physical growth, set of beliefs, human behavior, genetic information, and the way we perceive reality is just a part of ourselves, represented in a tangible practical way through the physical body.

If anyone needs to improve an area to adapt to social interaction, they tend to rely first on the ways to approach a new system, this might be such as belonging to a religious community, to become a club member, or to go to a gym to gain muscular tone.

The intention to accomplish any of these goals start first on wondering how to reach a goal, which starts as an idea to process a linear or non-linear thinking. Transmutation from thought to action helps brain plasticity, which is the brain's ability to change behavior throughout life, making more cognitive tools available.

Recent research has shown that, under the right circumstances, the power of brain plasticity can help minds grow in people of all ages.[1] From the action phase, the mind comes into focus, to connect perception, beliefs, behavior, and reality. But the result, the ultimate change, begins at the mind's screen.

We visualize what we want our future to be like, and we mentally program ourselves to visualize an unmanifested movie of our life, blending our subconscious abilities, such as social adaptability, our oral and nonverbal communication skills, and our sense of fight or flight as a survival tool, by the way we perceive and visualize reality through our senses.[2]

The growing understanding and interest in brain plasticity is driving a scientific revolution that measures how the brain changes anatomically by the way we perceive and visualize through our senses. The scientific community has discovered through observation that neuroplasticity is related to memory and cognition.[3]

Imagine what your life would be like if you had no ability to remember what you did early in the morning or the day before, or if you were unable to memorize a phone number, or understand a directive from your employer, or try as you might you could not recognize the faces of your family or friends. Without learning or maintaining a lucid memory, the simplest task becomes complex and irrelevant.[4]

Much effort, time and financial resources have been invested in the quest to study the brain to understand how it works. Physicists have developed new tools, classified under the acronyms MRI, EEG, PET, CAT, MSCT, TES and DBS, for the sole purpose of learning more about the human body. Extraordinary studies and amazing findings have been made about the brain using appropriate scientific methods to reveal the thoughts that are activated in a living, thinking brain.

Just as the lungs are the organs in charge of oxygenating the blood, the brain is the organ in charge of remembering past experiences and learning new tasks. This amazing organ oversees storing all the information that makes you, you; your name, where you live, the faces you know, your talents and skills, your area of expertise, etc.).

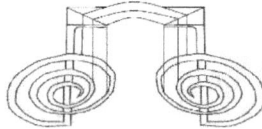

CHAPTER TWO

BROKEN BRAINS

"According to the inscription on Dr. Mikao Usui's tombstone, it shows that he taught Reiki to over 2000 people during his lifetime. Sixteen of these students continued their training until they reached the Shinpiden[1] (Mysterious Teaching) level, which is the equivalent of the Western third degree or Master level. Dr. Usui died on March 9, 1926, from a stroke."[2]

When a stroke occurs, it is because the brain does not receive enough oxygen or nutrients necessary for its functioning, resulting in the death of brain cells. *Strokes* occur because of problems in the blood supply to the brain, either because the blood supply is blocked or because a blood vessel within the brain ruptures.

A brain attack or stroke, is the most common brain disorder, also known as a cerebrovascular accident (CVA).

A CVA is characterized by abrupt onset of persisting neurological symptoms, such as paralysis or loss of sensation, which arises from destruction of the brain tissue.

Common causes of a stoke are:

- intracerebral hemorrhage, from a blood vessel in the pia matter or brain,

- emboli caused by blood clots, and

- atherosclerosis of the cerebral arteries, which is the formation of cholesterol-containing plaques that block blood flow.[3]

The risk factors of a CVA are high blood pressure, high blood cholesterol, heart disease, narrowed carotid arteries, transient ischemic attacks (TIAs), diabetes, smoking, obesity, and excessive alcohol intake.[4]

CVAs affect 500,000 people each year in the United States representing the third most deadly illness, behind heart attacks and cancer; other sources show that approximately 800,000 experience a stroke each year.[5]

Reasons why a stroke may happen

- Because the brain does not receive enough oxygen or nutrients, causing brain cells to die.[6]

- There are three main kinds of stroke: ischemic strokes, hemorrhagic strokes, and transient ischemic attacks (TIA).

- Ischemic strokes are caused by a narrowing or blocking of arteries to the brain.[7]

- A TIA is an episode of temporary brain dysfunction caused by altered blood flow to the brain, usually persisting for 5 to 10 minutes and rarely lasting 24 hours. It does not leave permanent neurological disorders. Its symptoms include weakness, numbness, dizziness, or paralysis in one limb or on one side of the body; headache; drooping of one side of the face; speech impediment or difficulty in understanding what is heard; and partial loss of vision or the presence of double vision. Sometimes nausea or vomiting also occurs.[8]

- Hemorrhagic strokes are caused by blood vessels in and around the brain bursting or leaking.

- Strokes need to be diagnosed and treated as quickly as possible to minimize brain damage.

Tissue plasminogen activator (t-PA), a clot -dissolving drug is now being used to open blocked blood vessels in the brain, being most effective when administered *within three hours* of the onset of the CVA. This clot dissolving drug can decrease the permanently disability associated with these types of CVAs by 50%. "New studies show that "cold therapy" might be successful by limiting the amount of a residual CVA damage. States of hypothermia seem to trigger a survival response in which the body requires less oxygen. Some commercial companies now are providing "CVA survival kits," which include cooling blankets that can be kept at home,[9] but regardless of new preventive ways to deal with a stroke, only a qualified physician may apply the right treatment depending on the type of stroke.[10]

The need to observe the scientific method

"A story on Reiki energy therapy in Your Health Oct. 23, 2001, incorrectly stated that a government-funded Reiki study on stroke patients showed that the therapy helped reduce stroke disability in the first year."

"The study's principal investigator Samuel Shiflett, who conducted the study at the Kessler Medical Rehabilitation Research & Education Corp. in West Orange, N.J., said last week the therapy did not help in stroke recovery. Elena Gillespie, a Reiki Master and University of Michigan Medical Center researcher who provided the reporter with information about the Kessler

> *study, said in reading the study's results, she believed Reiki provided some help with pain management."[11]*

According to the note published on *post-gazette.com*, although Reiki provided some help with pain management, did not "helped reduce stroke disability in the first year."

I'm sure there is much to observe and work on other diseases when applying and working with the universal energy. Research and data banks need to be observed when doing Reiki sessions as reference for future interventions.

Neuroscientists support the idea of neuroplasticity and that in certain parts of the brain reside the emotions that interconnect human behavior patterns. This discovery is not new, the scientific community has been aware of it since 1860, after Dr. John Harlow studied the brain of Phineas Gage, who in 1848 was involved in an explosion, in which the prefrontal part of the brain was severely affected by an iron bar that pierced the occipital bone, landing the iron bar twenty-two meters away. Fortunately, Gage did not die from the impact, but until 1860, but his behavior changed radically making him "capricious and indecisive" according to Harlow.

Reiki was brought to the West by Hawayo Takata, known in Japan as an ancient healing system. Takata learned Reiki after a serious illness with little chance of regaining health. She was admitted to the clinic of Hayashi, who provided, upon request, healing sessions to those in need. Takata learned the basic Usui hand positions from Hayashi. Hayashi also learned the hand positions from Dr. Mikao Usui, a person who was granted the vision, perception, and ability to transmit such Universal Energy to everyone

Unconditional love is the key to giving Reiki, along with the desire to learn a deep knowledge of human anatomy and physiology, as well as balancing the four bodies, which are: the mental body, the psychological body, and the spiritual body, all contained in the physical body. Reiki is a shortcut to access universal energy and the results of its applications are easy to achieve. The benefits are received with the attunement necessary to succeed in any illness treated, by observing the precepts of Reiki and detachment from the ego of believing that by being the conduit of energy one can dominate the balances of the universal energy.

Although every human being is born with this Universal Energetic Force contained in a spark, whose properties and scope are often ignored, forgotten, or never known. Human beings are born and can learn where they come from, what tools or abilities they have been granted and how to use them, but who could teach about this unknown and difficult to understand power through logic?

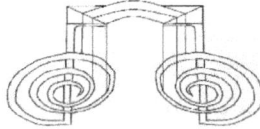

CHAPTER THREE

REIKI RULES TO KEEP GROWTH AND DISCIPLINE

Reiki is based on a set of rules, rituals, and procedures. When Reiki was instituted, it was necessary to be part of a new set of rules.

Masters who shared these gifts followed a way to keep their knowledge safe and untainted.

Reiki Master Jean Ferris guided us all on the protocol of rules to be observed while practicing the Reiki symbols, and during the teaching on hand positions, she remained open to review in depth the questions that were rumbling in the minds of the students. All the doubts I had about energetic balancing were cleared, and I followed the rules as instructed to the students to maintain the balance of what was learned.

Things were running smooth by that time. My spirits were growing strong, and every Sunday was expected like a new coming opportunity, like a new sunset to embrace after the joy of having watched a Sunrise, until the threads of doubt started showing within the local Reiki community. Through the grapevine, we heard Reiki Grand Master Phyllis Lei Furumoto, Takata's granddaughter, was about to be removed from the Reiki Alliance by an antagonist group, the same group initiated by Takata years before. It was known to me that a similar event had happened years before but hearing such a story confused the students who attended the Sunday classes of teacher Jean Ferris in El Paso, Texas.

It is quite possible that this information was mistakenly revealed to the group of students who met weekly at the home of Reiki Master Usui Jean Ferris, as it had happened fifteen years earlier -1983/1999- but the desire to learn the transmission of Reiki energy clouded the group's ability to investigate, choosing to believe a rumor.

But deep down, the Ferris student group was unsure whether to believe the rumors about the dismissal of Grand Master Phyllis Furumoto in the 1990s, as a similar event had occurred in the 1980s, when the Takata student group had split into three branches. The group I was attending needed more information on the subject, but what was going on within the Reiki Alliance was treated with secrecy, and sensitive issues were not public.

In between, the lack of informational continuity began to crack our peace of mind, without ending in total ruin. Our leader, Phyllis Furumoto, whom I had never met, "was about to be ousted from her throne, from a realm she had never known in El Paso, Texas."

Following a leader is a two-way commitment. The leader is indirectly responsible for his or her actions, and the followers are also responsible for their own actions. From these two variables, with their interaction, followers make a leader. The presence of a leader is realized through the obedience and submission of the followers to the leader's ideals. When the nature of the leader is at play, the follower's system begins to tremble, until it breaks down. Based on the outcome, the follower can either polarize to disbelief or reinforce his or her values.

In our case we didn't fall apart about the unclear situation of our leader Phyllis Furumoto, Reiki Master of the Reiki Alliance, for Reiki's love embraces polarities as a balance. Master Ferris did a great job teaching us well when telling us about the power of the symbols. In this case, if the rumors heard had triggered an emotional outburst in the students, the use of symbols would reduce their impending devastating effects.

Sunrise after Confusion

After overcoming the gossip about the removal of the leader of the Reiki Alliance, time passed without any news.

Three months later, while visiting my friend Lydia's home, she mentioned that she had had contact with Grandmaster Furumoto by phone. Lydia shared this news to the rest of the group and excitement began to grow among all the Reiki practitioners, as Lydia had mentioned that Phyllis Lei Furumoto had a list of all of Master Ferris' practitioners.

Lydia's information was corroborated at the weekly meeting the following Sunday afternoon. Reiki Master Jean Ferris mentioned that Grand Master Phyllis Lei Furumoto would be contacting all of Jean's students to update them on the latest news and updates on Usui's Reiki.

On further talks with Lydia, she told me that Furumoto was going to take charge of the El Paso Reiki region, overseeing Master Ferris's instruction. This information changed the whole picture of things so, many of Ferris' students stop attending her teaching facility, including Lydia and myself. This were terrible news, and very sad. And the saddest part of this situation is that I did not have the opportunity and the courage to corroborate such information with other students in the group that Lydia and I attended on Sunday afternoons.

Although Jean Ferris was my Reiki Usui teacher, it did not cross my mind to clarify these doubts with her.

Sometimes having a leader in high esteem, makes it difficult to approach him/her, because of the lack of conviction to play the role of student/teacher, because I should had remembered, that teachers are here to guide our learning and clarify all doubts.

Direct Bearer of the Usui Healing System

As announced, Usui Shiki Ryoho Grand Master, Phyllis Lei Furumoto visit came to effect. First and second Reiki level Practitioners were invited to talk to her or at least meet in person this legendary figure.

Reiki Grand Master's arrival was exciting for Reiki practitioners who were expecting her visit eagerly. Phyllis addressed all the practitioners with respect but stay away from central Reiki conversations. Guests were savoring a variety of dishes brought to the event, but I noticed Gran Master Furumoto avoided to try any of the dishes brought by her followers to this so important and long- awaited event.

Lydia had told me that Phyllis' visit was mainly to weigh the possibility to take charge of the El Paso's Reiki Chapter, this shocking issue was never brought to the meeting. Master Jean Ferris didn't attend to the gathering. Master Phyllis presence was kind of reserved although she seemed confident and relaxed. She answered to trivial questions about the weather in Hawaii or about her next presentation stop. Master Phyllis peacefully left a couple of hours later, leaving a wonderful feeling on all attendees to the event.

No pictures were taken on this occasion, nobody thought about it, and I didn't asked Lydia if she had taken any photographs for, she was the host of such event. Reiki Grand Master Phyllis Lei Furumoto presence stayed in our hearts and in our minds, like if it were a dream... a good dream.

Phyllis Furumoto, Bearer of a Bifurcated Energy Realm

Lydia and I made some comments about Grand Master's visit, she seemed quiet but smiley. After Lydia and I had exhausted perceptual insights, we shared farewell to one another and promised to meet later. This never happened, for time passed and I moved months later to Phoenix. Twelve years had passed, haven't talked to each other since.

Through the internet, I read that the Reiki Alliance had split into two different groups in 1982. Keeping Phyllis Furumoto, the title of Reiki

Grand Master in front of the Reiki Alliance, and an opposite group who claimed to embrace the right to called themselves the bearers of Takata's direct and real Reiki teachings. The system Radiance Technique International Association Inc. (TRTIA) was born under the leadership of Reiki Master Dr. Barbara Weber Ray.[1]

Rippled Action Effects

When a butterfly in China beats its wings, its besting bounces aerial ripples to the rest of the world.

You won't notice this ripple effect, but if you develop a connection with subtle energy this wing beating will resonate within yourself.

Likewise, the emotional ripple created by Reiki Grand Master Phyllis Furumoto's chain of events released a sort of restricted information kept within the Reiki Alliance's bosom; just like the vibrational structure of the Universal Force, interweaved in the original attunements passed on to Dr. Usui at Mount Kurama, are still spreading a ripple effect and opening its healing proprieties to the needy.

Information just like healing energy proprieties, are like boiling water kept on a container which must find its way out, with a hissing sound releasing it or with a thunderous explosion.

A revealing occurrence released in the heart of the Reiki Alliance unknown to its followers was freed with a muffled rumbling, touching the souls of millions of *Universal Force* seekers.

According to speculation fifteen years ago - in 1983/1999 - the break occurred, in part, because Second Level Reiki practitioners wanted to receive the Master Degree from Grandmaster Furumoto, who believed that granting Third Level Reiki Master/Practitioner attunements implied a period of time to be prepared to honor the teachings of Reiki as a way of life, and that practitioners needed to understand that all who had received the attunements needed to be prepared to honor the teachings of Reiki as a way of life; and that practitioners needed to understand that all who had received attunements were to dedicate their lives to the practice and teachings of Reiki as a lifelong commitment.

The practitioners felt that their requests were unnecessarily held back from becoming part of their life purpose, so they chose a way to receive the Third Level Reiki Master/Teacher/Practitioner from another source.

I do not fully know if the events that occurred after 1983 loomed to be repeated in 1999, -when I received my initiations from Master Ferris-this remains hidden in the eternal annals of the Reiki Alliance.

Universal Life Force for All

In 1975,[2] after pressure from some students to receive the Reiki Master Symbol attunements, Takata - the Third Grand Reiki Master - began to bestow the Reiki Master Symbols on non-conforming candidates. Before she passed away, Mrs. Hawayo Takata awarded the Reiki Master level symbols to twenty-two Reiki students,[3] who in turn initiated other candidates.

Here are the names of the twenty-two Reiki Masters initiated by Reiki Master Hawayo Takata:

- George Araki

- Dorothy Baba

- Ursula Baylow

- Rick Bockner

- Patricia Bowling

- Barbara Brown

- Fran Brown

- Phyllis Lei Furumoto

- Beth Gray

- John Harvey Gray

- Iris Ishikuro

- Harry M. Kuboi

- Ethel Lombardi

- Barbara Lincoln McCullough

- Mary Alexandra McFadyen

- Paul Mitchell

- Bethal Phaigh

- Shinobu Saito

- Virginia W. Samdahl

- Wanja Twan

- Barbara Weber

- Kay Yamashita[4]

Reiki Masters became ordained all around the world. Reiki became so popular for its soothing effects and healing proprieties that everyone wanted its share of this heavenly blessing.

Schools bloomed around the world, but at the beginning the few started to spread their influence claiming to be bearers of the true Dr. Mikao Usui's teachings for it came directly from Hawayo Takata's legacy. Everyone wanted to spread this knowledge to the world. No one before Mrs. Takata had taught Reiki outside of Japan, and this occurred due to the conditions on the island after World War II. She brought the Usui lineage to the West and developed it into Usui Reiki, the predominant modality of energy work that continues to grow in popularity and is practiced throughout the world. The turmoil left by World War II caused other forms of Reiki to fall into disuse and remain relatively unknown[5] or kept secret.

Because to Usui Reiki's exposure, a clear and deep understanding of this modality provided a basis for understanding its five admonitions and empowering uses, making it easier for the world to embrace its essence.

According to Hiroshi Doi Sensei and Toshitaka Mochitzuki Sensei, there were at least four other Reiki healing modalities used in Japan by 1922, and according to Reiki researchers, it was Mataji Kawakami, who truly created Reiki in 1914.

Mikao Usui's Reiki promotes peace and harmony that through Hayashi's teachings and his clinical applications to energy receptors, has acquired a sub-atomic healing code to be imprinted in the patient's mind, on an emotional level, permeating spiritual thoughts and reconnecting the memory of physical cells. Today, Reiki is used in many different cultures and is therefore not considered a religion.

The need to spread this pure realm was sincere to some Reiki Masters; although Reiki attunements became the media to reach energy power and inner balance, the financial appeal also started to raise along its divulgation. Greed was also an ingredient for the teacher guild appearance avalanche, and because every new branch claimed to be the original bearers of such knowledge, some started to stress differences in their teaching and style expertise.

Some Reiki Masters saw a chance to grow financially so they started to charge the stated fares for the official Reiki attunement rituals according Takata's fixed prices for the first ($150.00), second ($500.00), and third Reiki levels ($10,000.00 USD).

Today in the year 2022, the prices offered by instructors to offer Reiki courses are different. There are several types of presentations such as video courses lasting up to two (2) hours for $300.00; online classes lasting 3-5 hours for $395.00 and in-person courses lasting 3-5 hours for $400.00.

Today's prices, compared to the rates charged by the Reiki Alliance or other associations derived from the Usui system, make a big difference in price, but certainly, the difference is also in the quality of knowledge and service.

The first level course taught by a Traditional Usui Reiki Master has a duration of about 18 hours. The course is given on a weekend, on Friday with 4 hours and on Saturday and Sunday with 8 hours per day. The same length of hours applies to the second level and mastery courses. Other Reiki modalities also offer courses with the same duration of hours and on the same days, charging for each course, 1st level, 2nd level, and 3rd level or mastery $150.00 each. Today remote sessions can also range from $20.00 to $120.00 with a duration varying from 10 to 45 minutes.

There are no official prices for services provided because every Reiki practitioner and teacher is trying to make their own way in these difficult financial times.

The inconsistency of prices per facilitated service, and the difference in prices and time in the delivery of courses, makes this discipline an unserious modality in the eyes of skeptics and scientists of the profession.

The lack of data where the advances and results of the applications of the energetic sessions are registered, and the registration of practitioners, teachers, and schools, within official groups, are necessary to give strength to the seriousness of the Reiki disciplines and modalities. The first step has been taken, to generate interest in the community to know, learn and practice the management of vital energy; the rest will come as well.

Let's go back a little bit, and stress that Reiki is the Universal Life Force, and coming from the first bearer Mikao Usui,[6] where at Mount Kurama he received the blessing of Life Force represented by strokes of light[7] and the symbols to be shared to all living creatures in the universe. Reiki contains all the power of the universe within, and its influence will vibrate if the symbols and teachings are unveiled to eager soul seekers.

Usui taught the Reiki principle to 2000 persons, and initiated 21 students,[8] one of whom is Dr. Chujiro Hayashi who treated a patient in need, Hawayo Takata from asthma and gall stones, daily for three weeks at Hayashi's clinic.

27

After Dr. Hayashi treated and healed Takata, he wanted to learn Reiki. Takata received attunements from Dr. Chujiro Hayashi, bringing to the West the possibility of a relationship with this energy, through Reiki Usui Shiki Ryoho[9], a word translated from Japanese as *Universal Life Energy*.

Reiki before Mikao Usui

According to thorough research done by Reiki Master William Lee Rand "in 1914, Matiji Kawakami, a Japanese therapist, created a healing style he called Reiki Ryoho and in 1919, he published a book titled *Reiki Ryoho to Sono Koka*, or *Reiki Healing and Its Effects*. The other Reiki healing styles in use at the time were: Reikan Tonetsu Ryoho created by Reikaku Ishinuki, Senshinryu Reiki Ryoho created by Kogetsu Matsubara and Seido Reishojutsu created by Reisen Oyama. It was during the time that these Reiki styles were already in use that in March 1922, Usui Sensei had his mystical experience on Kurama Yama in which he was given the Reiki energy and from this developed his style of Reiki, which he called Usui Reiki Ryoho. It is interesting that Usui Sensei chose this name as it tends to indicate that he knew of the other styles of Reiki Ryoho in use and was indicating that this was his style of Reiki Ryoho." [10] [11]

Mataji Kawakami
Created Reiki Ryoho in 1914.
Author of Reiki Healing and Its
Effects *Published 1919.*

However, because of conditions in Japan after World War II and the fact that Hawayo Takata had brought Reiki to the west, Usui Reiki became the predominate form of Reiki practiced throughout the world. Because of this, a thorough understanding of Usui Reiki is important as it will give us a foundation for understanding Reiki, making it easier for us to connect with its essence."[12]

Through the statement above, we may see that the manifestations of Universal Energy have been in the energy grid for centuries, it is because of the special spirited persons that these fields are tuned into by resonance and downloaded to the third dimension. While in this dimension the spiritual resonances are classified and structured for further teachings, and data.

In March 1922,[13] Mikao Usui, received the attributions of power while meditating at Mount Kurama. Universal Energy transfer system was received by thousands of Usui's followers and so far, thousands of supporters have engaged in it. Mrs. Takata first introduced Reiki to the U.S., in the 1970's, through the transfer of powers received by master Chujiro Hayashi.

The way of how the Reiki system is carried out is by receiving the empowerment through traditional lineage, which allegedly started by Mikao Usui. For a person to receive the empowerment of the traditional Reiki system, it must be through a qualified teacher belonging to the traditional Reiki Usui system. The transfer of power takes place orally by a third level Reiki Master through a series of initiations for the attribution of powers which are invested in the practitioner for the conduction of universal energy.

The investiture of power ranks the student's energy system, giving them the ability to be able to self - treat and align an energy field and at the same time, to balance the energetic field of others through the laying-on of hands at certain points in the physical body. The Reiki System Usui Shiki Ryoho was developed by Dr. Usui, but it was Dr. Hayashi who developed the 12 basic Reiki hand positions introducing a formal approach to clinical Reiki.[14] Mrs. Takata's healing sessions were done based on an intuitive healing approach, which according to her, she was never taught hand positions.[15]

After Mrs. Takata death in 1980,[16] the Usui system was formalized by giving a solid structure to this form of energy transfer practice, but in a first Assembly formed by 22 teachers and practitioners, all Mrs. Takata's students in the year of 1982, by differences of opinions decided to branch the Usui system into two recognized systems and a third one made up of independent practitioners.[17]

One of these systems, the Reiki Alliance, was represented in 1983, by Mrs. Takata's granddaughter, Phyllis Lei Furumoto; this Reiki system consisting of three levels with the investiture of four symbols. The sector of the Reiki Alliance adopted a new field by formulating this creed:

"We are an Alliance of Reiki Masters. We regard all masters as equal in the oneness of Reiki. We acknowledge Phyllis Lei Furumoto as a Grand Master in the direct spiritual lineage of Mikao Usui, Chujiro

Hayashi, and Hawayo Takata. The purpose of the alliance is to support us as teachers in the Usui System of natural Healing."[18]

Phyllis Furumoto became an honorary member of P*roReiki*, a German organization. In her acceptance speech in 2014, Furumoto manifested her openness towards different practices and a totally conciliatory spirit. This was a moment of inspiration for the realization of *Reconciliation.*[19]

† *On March 31, 2019, Phyllis Lei Furumoto transitioned her earthly life in Green Valley, Arizona. Recognizing two weeks prior to her transition, as her successor, Johannes Reindl. Phyllis Lei Furumoto left an indelible memory in the world of Reiki, in the hearts of many students, friends, and colleagues.*

† *Reiki Master, Jean Ferris, passed away on August 16, 2015, at her home in Texas. Leaving in the hearts of all the students who attended her Sunday classes in El Paso, Texas, an indelible memory.*

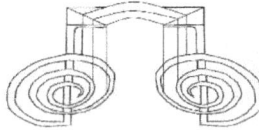

CHAPTER FOUR

RECREATING DR. MIKAO USUI'S REIKI

Seekers Finding Their Own Way

The system Radiance Technique International Association Inc. (TRTIA) also emerged from Mrs. Takata teachings, and is headed by Dr. Barbara Weber Ray, who stated that it was Takata herself who had given her most of the symbolic tools, to better deal with the Reiki Master level, compared to the other disciples.[1]

This system consists of seven levels[2] offering different symbols and additional methods. Barbara Weber received her third-degree initiation in 1979, directly from Ms. Takata.[3]

On TRITA's electronic portal, it is stipulated that only those initiated under the direction of the company possess the true and original teachings of Takata.[4]

It was not earlier to 1988, that the Reiki Alliance recognized as its only Reiki Master, Phyllis Lei Furumoto as the Lineage Bearer of Usui Shiki Ryoho (Usui System of Natural Healing), in charge to initiate new

Reiki Masters. Due to pressure upon requests to receive the endowment of third-level powers or Reiki Masters, Furumoto announced that every Master with the necessary knowledge and experience[5] could bestow to others the third-level degree.

This initiative, by the only one with authority to grant other Reiki Masters and Practitioners to initiate others to the master's level, opened the doors of abundance by where it became a torrent of new Reiki teachers over a few years.[6]

This separation of ideologies, which starting from one, turned up to become two official different fields. From these change, two distinct practices emerged, one emphasizing the four aspects of the practice and the other concentrated on the healing technique.[7]

And from this development of divisions were created a series of polarities, all positive from a point of view, but unilateral without realizing that the counterpart could see differently from the other. One point of view antagonistic to each other, with 51% in opposition to each other. Thus, creating a dissonance, an inner fear of not being right according to the other.

The Reiki Usui system has become very popular nowadays and practiced by millions of people worldwide, and due to its popularity, such system of universal energy transference has generated other variants of this energy modality, among which can be counted more than 112 different Reiki modalities. [8] [9]

Here is a compendium of Reiki modalities, which due to the volatile nature of energy fields, keeps expanding:

Reiki Modalities

1. Adama Starfire Reiki,	57. Lightarian Reiki,
2. Ahara Reiki,	58. Lunar/Solar Light Empowerment,
3. Aloha Reiki,	59. Magnusa Phoenix Reiki,
4. Alef Reiki,	60. Mari El Reiki,
5. Alchemy Reiki,	61. Medicine Buddha Reiki,
6. Amanohuna Reiki,	62. Medicine Dharma Reiki (Men Chho Reiki),
7. Amara Omni Empowerment Reiki,	63. Medicine Reiki,
8. Amonohuna Reiki,	64. Monastic Seven Degree Reiki,
9. Ancient Egipcian Reiki,	65. Money Reiki,
10. Angelic Reiki,	66. New Life Reiki,
11. Anugraha Reiki,	67. Ni Kawa Reiki,
12. Aromatherapy Reiki,	68. Orb of Life,
13. Ascencsion Reiki,	69. Osho Neo Reiki,
14. Authentic Reiki,	70. Pyramid Reiki,
15. Awen Energy Transformation,	71. Ra Sheeba,
16. Blue Star Reiki,	72. Radiance Technique,
17. Brahma Satya Reik,	73. Rainbow Reiki,
18. Buddho Ennersense Reiki,	74. Raku Kei Reiki,
19. Byosen Reikan Ho,	75. Raku Reiki,
20. Celestial Reiki,	76. Reikan Tonetsu Ryoho,
21. Celtic Reiki,	77. Reiki Essential,
22. Chikara-Reiki-Do,	78. Reiki, Kundalini Reiki I,
23. Chios Energy Healing Reiki,	79. Reiki, Kundalini Reiki II,
24. *Crown ReiQi©*,	80. Reiki Plus,
25. Crystal Reiki,	81. Reiki Tummo,
26. Dorhe Reiki,	82. Reiki Unitario,
27. Dos Rios Reiki	83. Reiki Usui Tibetano,
28. Dragon Reiki,	84. Run Valdr,
29. Elemental Reiki,	85. Sacred Flames Reiki,
30. Elven Shamanic Healing,	86. Sacred Path Reiki,
31. Ethereal Crystals Gold Reiki,	87. Sai Baba Reiki,
32. Faery Reiki,	88. Saku Reiki,
33. Fire Serpent Reiki,	89. Sands of Egypt
34. Fusion Reiki,	90. Sangle Mendela Reiki Do,
35. Gakkai Reiki,	91. Satya Japanese Reiki,

36. Gendai Reiki,	92. Shakyamuni Reiki,
37. Golden Age Reiki,	93. Shambhala Reiki,
38. Hayashi Reiki Ryoho,	94. Shambala Multi-Dimensional Healing,
39. Hypno Reiki,	95. Siddhearta Reiki,
40. Huna Reiki,	96. Silverwolf Reiki,
41. Ichi Sekai Reiki,	97. Seichim or Seichem Reiki
42. Imara Reiki,	98. Sun Li Chung Reiki,
43. Innersun Reiki,	99.Tanaki Reiki,
44. Japanese Reiki,	100. Tera-Mai Seichim,
45. Jikiden Reiki,	101. Tibetan Reiki,
46. Jinlap Maitre Reiki,	102. Tibetan Soul Star Reiki,
47. Johrei Reiki,	103. Universal Rays,
48. Karmic Reiki,	104. Universal Reiki Dharma,
49. Karuna Reiki,	105. Usui-Do,
50. Ken Reiki Do,	106. Usui reiki Ryoho Gakkai,
51. Ki Manna, Kava,	107. Usui Reiki,
52. Kurama Yama Reiki,	118. Violet Flame Reiki,
53. Kyra Reiki,	109. Violet Light Reiki,
54. Reiki Grand Master,	110. Wei Chi Tibetan Reiki,
55. Reiki Ho,	111. White Dove Reiki,
56. Reiki Jin Kei Do,	112. Wonderful Egyptian Style Reiki.

From this list, it can be seen there is a lot of symbols as part of the Reiki rituals; these symbols represent a story, a system, a field, and most of them have geometric shapes.

Apparently, all Reiki modalities differ from one another, and the spiritual progress provided to every teacher by the universal energy is based on a constant practice, which accomplishment endorses a sincere teaching with a unique style and technique.

Every teacher, third, second or first level Reiki practitioner, is vested with the lineage through the Reiki initiations, and with each session, the Universal Life Force is strengthened and consolidated by the all-time predecessor master.

Healing the Physical Body First, the Rest will Follow

Mikao Usui, according to some historians, read about the miracles Jesus did by laying on hands and healing the sick, as well as mentioned on the Buddhist Sutras or the Buddhist Bible where it notes that Buddha had healed leprosy, tuberculosis, and the blind, by laying on of hands.[10]

Usui had heard from the Buddhist monks it was more important to first straighten the minds of the people, so they'll become more spiritual and then, show more gratitude and learn all the better things in life. The Monks had told Usui, that they didn't have time to teach the people how to deal with the physical to accomplish spiritual growth; "spiritual healing is supposed to be taking care of first, they insisted."[11]

Mikao Usui wanted to heal the physical body and ease the pain people were experiencing due to illness, as mentioned in Usui's story about healing himself after the symbols were bestowed on him while meditating at Mont Kurama in March of 1922.[12]

Reiki, is a Japanese word which means, "mysterious atmosphere, miraculous sign."

Is formed by two words: Rei "soul, spirit" and Ki, which together will mean "vital energy."

According to the Sino-Japanese reading of Chinese língqì (靈氣) means: "numinous atmosphere." [13]

The Japanese Reiki is commonly written as レイキ in katakana syllabary or as 霊気 in shinjitai "new character form" kanji. It compounds the words Rei (霊): spirit, miraculous, divine, and Ki (気) qi: gas, vital energy, breath of life, consciousness. [14] [15]

Reiki's benefits:

- Reiki's manifestation vibrates on the same field of love and compassion Dr. Usui embraced within himself during all his life.

- Reiki comes from the void of superstrings.

- Reiki embraces a mystery outcome of events, all to benefit the receiver's expectations.

- A Reiki session benefits both the recipient and the conduit at the same time.

- Reiki for its high vibrational qualities unlocks blockages in a living body.[16]

Although Reiki has shown to thousands of people its connectedness to a source which provides balance and relaxation, the medical guild has stated that Reiki is considered a practice which outcome cannot be proven as facts. The allopathic medical field considers Reiki as alternative medicine identified as a pseudoscience.[17] It is based on qi-chi-, which practitioners say is a *Universal Life Force*, although there is no empirical evidence that such a life force exists.[18][19] Clinical research has not shown Reiki to be effective as a medical treatment for any medical condition.[20] The American Cancer Society,[21] Cancer Research UK,[22] and the National Center for Complementary and Integrative Health[23] state that Reiki should not be a replacement for conventional treatments.

Considering the above statement as a partial point of view outspoken by official speakers from the medical field, it's admissible as an authentic point of view, for any medical treatment should always be supervised by the prime care physician, and Reiki or any other energy work modality should complement a medical or counseling treatment.

According to the definition of alternative medicine we may see there are two different sides to a definition applied to this practice, which may be considered a practice orbiting the borders of the medical discipline without getting to intertwine with.

Alternative medicine consists of practices claimed to have healing effects, but not able to be proven according to the standards of the medical field. Healing effects through the practice of hands-on imposition are disproved, unproven, impossible to prove or are excessively harmful in relation to their effect; this based on the standards of a scientific consensus.

A scientific consensus is effective, when according to proven data gathered through a huge number of people is dedicated to repeat the laws of nature, by the different fields of science subjected to the scientific method principle. By trial and error, scientists have repeatedly tested on millions of people for success accomplishments and shown, proved, and repeated through data, the way to identify the health inalienable right every human has in life.

The medical guild has argued the alternative medicine therapy Reiki practitioners perform "does not or cannot work because, the known laws of nature are violated by its basic claims." [24]

The term wellness may be used to mean a state beyond absence of illness, illness as the lay refer to it as the absence of wellbeing or health. Important point to be mentioned is that Reiki's purpose is to provide wellness through Universal Energy considering this as an abstract field of Vital Energy. Vital Energy could be classified as Alternative medicine, to what medicine could be classified as conventional medicine. *Medicine is the science and art dealing with the maintenance of health and the prevention, alleviation, or cure of disease.*[25] This brings us to a question about this definition, if medicine is art, is Reiki a form of an artistic practice? If Reiki is energy, is medicine energy too? Well, according to some experienced Reiki practitioners Reiki is Energy Medicine.[26]

According to Libby Barnett and Maggie Chambers,[27] some medical institutions have invited them to teach an in-service Reiki program, or have suggested that they document their medical staff [28] to learn a method to complement their medical skills and, at the same time, receive an invaluable tool for their own health maintenance, self-renewal and personal growth.

Institutions like The Harvard Community Health Plan; the medical Center of Central Massachusetts; Cedarcrest Residential Center for Children with Disabilities; Concord Regional VNA-Hospice House;

Wentworth-Douglas Hospital, Dover, NH; Androscoggin Home Health services, Lewiston, ME; Englewood Hospital and Medical Center, Englewood, NJ; VNA of the Greater Milford/Northbridge Area, Mendon, VA; Emerson Hospital, Concord, MA; Healthcare Therapy Services, Indianapolis, IN; New London Hospital, NH; and Southwest New Hampshire Medical Center; are some institutions interested in providing a soothing alternative to patients through Reiki.[29]

Based on research on Integrative Medicine about the institutions mentioned I found out that most of them have a wellness Center where Reiki sessions, amongst other disciplines are provided. The Graf Center, for Integrative Medicine through the Englewood Hospital and Medical Center, Englewood, NJ. Still provides *Reiki sessions* daily;[30] the medical Center of Central Massachusetts, also provides *Reiki sessions* as needed; the Emerson Hospital, Concord, MA., also provides a wellness program where *Chi kung*, *Tai Chi*, *Nia*, Essentrics, Osteofitness, *Yoga*, *Gentle Pilates*, *Mindfulness Meditation*, and *Reiki* is provided.[31] Other medical institutions, although they have a Wellness Center program don't provide Reiki sessions such as the New London Hospital, NH.[32]

Energy Medicine's Setback Development

Medical authorities have claimed Reiki is considered so much worse than conventional treatment; that it would be unethical to offer as treatment. Alternative therapies or diagnoses are not part of medicine or science-based healthcare systems. According to opinions from the medical guild, Alternative medicine consists of a wide variety of practices, products, and therapies ranging from those that are biologically plausible but not well tested, to those with known harmful and toxic effects. [33] [34]

Let us be clear on this point, conventional medicine has been following a structural discipline reflected in its achievements, and consolidating its existence; alternative modalities on the other hand have not been following a structure based on scientific data, but this statement is becoming obsolete, as some schools of alternative modalities have begun to adapt structured and scientific fields, borrowing proven data from the beginning of the century of scientific fields, beginning to intertwine the denser fields with the subtle ones, a statement based on the principle that matter is made up of atoms, and atoms are electromagnetic fields. [35]

Contrary to what other scientific sources had established, complementary and Alternative medicine has kept records of scientific data based on their practices not only recently but registered since the Zhou Dynasty (1028-221 B.C.), being the first Imperial Dynasty to organize clinical medicine into separate divisions or medical departments. In the East every Dynasty had its own system for registering medical departments. The Imperial Medical colleges maintained several departments: Internal and External medicine including War Wounds, Fractures, Surgery, Traumatology, Ophthalmology, Pediatrics, Obstetrics, Abscesses and Ulcers, Diseases of the Mouth, Teeth and Throat, Dermatology and Antiseptic Techniques; Acupuncture and Moxibustion; Massage and Tissue Manipulation; Orthopedics; Oncology; Gynecology; Neurology; and Geriatrics.

On 16 November 2010, *UNESCO* declared moxibustion and Chinese acupuncture an Intangible Cultural Heritage of *Humanity*. [36]

Some medical areas were included in every Dynasty: The Zhou Dynasty, Northern Wei Dynasty of the Six Dynasties Periods (386-533 A.D.), Tang Dynasty (618- 907 A.D.), Song Dynasty (960-1279 A.D.), Yuan Dynasty (1279-1368 A.D.), Ming Dynasty (1368-1644 A.D.), Qing Dynasty (1644-1911 A.D.), The People's Republic of China (1949 A.D. -Present), all included this belief area on their services: Demonology; Charms and Incantations; Written Incantations; Prayers and Supplications; Acupuncture and Medical Chi kung Therapy.

After the Ming Dynasty (1368-1644 A.D.), it seemed the spiritual trend was separated from the scientific specialties being stressed after the Qing Dynasty (1644-1911 A.D.), not eradicated from its practice, but kept separated in another area: the mind and the spirit.

These came out to become part of the Traditional Chinese Medicine which included four branches: Acupuncture (including Needling, Cupping, Bloodletting, Moxa Burning, and magnet Healing).

Herbology and Dietetics (including Nutritional education; Teas and Soup; Tinctures and Wines; Oils, Balms, and liniments; and Compresses, Powders, and Pills); Massage Therapy (including Scraping Therapy, Tissue Manipulation, and Traumatology, Bone Setting, Visceral manipulation, and Channel Point Therapy); and Medical Qigong Therapy (including Qi Emission Therapy, Prescription Exercises and Meditations, Qigong Massage, Sound Therapy, and Invisible Needle Therapy).[37]

Most of these specialties are offered, and sometimes intermingled as a Traditional Alternative Medicine due its similar scientific foundation in Biology, and areas of specialization as Human Anatomy, Physiology, Pathology, and Histology all practiced by the medical guild.

Medical science covers many subjects which try to explain how the human body works. Starting with basic biology it is generally divided into areas of specialization such as anatomy, physiology and pathology included biochemistry, microbiology, molecular biology and genetics. Students and practitioners of the holistic health models also recognize the importance of the mind-body connection and the importance of nutrition.[38]

Many different areas make up the practice of complementary and alternative medicine (CAM). In addition, many parts of one field may overlap with the parts of another field. For example, acupuncture is also used in conventional medicine. In the U.S., -CAM is used by about 38% of adults and 12% of children. Examples of CAM include:

- Traditional Alternative Medicine (TAM). This field includes the conventional and most accepted forms of therapy, such as acupuncture, homeopathy, and Oriental practices. These therapies have been practiced for centuries worldwide. Traditional Alternative Medicine may include:

  o Acupuncture

  o Ayurveda

  o Homeopathy

  o Naturopathy

- o   Traditional Chinese or Oriental medicine

- o   Holistic Nursing

- **Body.** Touch has been used in medicine since the early days of medical care. Healing by touch is based on the idea that illness or injury in one area of the body can affect all parts of the body. If, with manual manipulation, the other parts can be brought back to optimum health, the body can fully focus on healing at the site of injury or illness. Body techniques are often combined with those of the mind. Examples of body therapies include:

  - o   Chiropractic and osteopathic medicine

  - o   Massage therapy

  - o   Body movement therapies

  - o   Chi kung

  - o   Tai chi

  - o   Yoga

  - o   Reflexology

- **Diet and herbs.** Over the centuries, man has gone from a simple diet consisting of meats, fruits, vegetables, and grains, to a diet that often consists of foods rich in fats, oils, and complex carbohydrates. Nutritional excess and deficiency have become problems today, both leading to certain chronic diseases. Many dietary and herbal approaches attempt to balance the body's nutritional well-being. Dietary and herbal approaches may include:

  - o   Dietary supplements

  - o   Herbal medicine

  - o   Nutrition/diet

- **Vital Energy.** Vital Energy or life force, according to Traditional Chinese Medicine-TCM- embraces all living creatures. Vital

Energy can be absorbed from nature, from the stars and planets and from the cosmos' void. Some people believe external energies from objects or other sources directly affect a person's health. An example of external energy therapy is:

- o Electromagnetic therapy

- o Reiki

- o Chi kung

- o Pellowah

- o Spiritual healing

- Mind. Even standard or conventional medicine recognizes the power of the connection between mind and body. Studies have found that people heal better if they have good emotional and mental health. Therapies using the mind may include:

  - o Transcendental Meditation (TM)

  - o Chi kung

  - o Biofeedback

  - o Hypnosis

  - o NLP

  - o EMDR

- Senses.[39] Some people believe the senses: touch or somatosensory, sight or vision, hearing or audition, smell or olfaction, taste, or gustation, vestibular, and proprioception, can affect overall health. Examples of therapies incorporating the senses include:

  - o Art, dance, and music

  - o Visualization and guided imagery

  - o Chi kung (Internal and External energy flow)[40]

Vital Energy can be developed, guided, and manipulated through energy work through different methods like Chi kung, T'ai Chi ch'uan, Chinese alchemy, Acupuncture and Hindu Yoga. According to these methods, Vital Energy flows within the human body through a channel network called *meridians* and its *collaterals*. These *meridians* and *collaterals* are connected to the inner organs of the body which through hand manipulation, sight, breath emission or the power the mind may balance the energy flow running in the *meridians*. Balancing the energy flow running within the energy channels may release energy blockages, adjust weak energy flow, and restore its strength to gain excellent health and peace of mind.

Such *meridian* network and *associated vessels* have been used for centuries by the countries in the East and in the World.

Despite satisfactory results while treating disease and terminal illnesses through Chi kung, Acupuncture and Chinese alchemy, some scientists do not accept acupuncture or Medical Qigong Therapy, primarily because the meridian system lacks a physical anatomical basis.

Scientific theories have not been able to explain the functional paths used by Traditional Eastern Medicine to cure physical disorders. According to Western medicine, -contrary of what TCM sustains- no known anatomical foundation exists for the meridians and unknown nervous, circulatory, endocrine, and immune mechanisms to mediate the effects of acupuncture or energy work.

The medical guild in its intent to narrow the gap between mind and spirit has followed other countries' scientific investigations like the research done by North Korea.[41]

Scientists in this country, after years of research, applied in one of their trials a blue dye in the energetic paths, observing an iridescence by photon emission, which with special technology was detected and photographed. This modality for detecting the meridians or energetic pathways in the body was called the *Primo Vascular System*.[42]

The *Primo Vascular System* (PVS) is a previously unknown system that harmonizes the functions of the eleven human body homeostatic systems. It also provides a physical substrate for the acupuncture points and meridians.

Conventional treatments are subjected for testing undesired side-effects, whereas *alternative treatments*, in general, are not subjected to such testing at all. Any treatment – whether conventional or alternative, that has a biological or psychological effect on a patient may also have potential to possess dangerous biological or psychological side-effects.

It has been noted that conventional treatments have taken a long route in the fight of some diseases, sometimes taking the longest route without a satisfactory end likewise, Alternative medicine modalities, just can't beat the dense atomic concentration of disease in the physical plane.

Conventional medicine has come a long way through trial and error. There are so many scientific fields working all together to fight a common enemy, diseases. Alternative energy modalities move on a different frequency. Energy vibrates in the spiritual and emotional bodies, while physical diseases belong to the world of the senses.

The senses belong to the physical world nevertheless, the senses perceive reality according to a program of logic and acculturation to fit a coherent behavior based on logic and ethics. The senses through electromagnetic impulses perceive reality,[43] translating these impulses as part of a set of laws of physics and mathematics which belong to a similar field as the ethereal field, untangled and indiscernible at simple observation, but when looked closely it will seem illogic.

The sight is perceived by photon impacts to the eyes by entering the eye and triggering chemical reactions in the retina, releasing through neuropeptides, electro-chemical impulses which travel along nerve fibers to the brain and to later -almost instantly, analyses the data it receives, and then creates its own picture of what is out there.[44] About sound, you may hear people talking in a restaurant or family members at home or listening to your favorite music on your *iPod*, all the sounds we hear is a communication process registered by trial and error in our mind. There is no sound as such in the external world, just vibrating air molecules,[45] just like striking a set of tubular bells with a mallet. Each tubular bell will vibrate differently due to its short-wave condition resonating in your ears and translating this vibration as sound.

Same thing will happen with our sense of smell, it is chemical molecules we taste which translates it as a different category of flavor, this may explain why we love cupcakes with a strawberry or vanilla artificial flavor.

With this at hand we may say that our human senses are deceiving us — maybe its existence is an illusion,[46] and reality isn't real, but it's real for you can feel and keep on living, connecting past events and wondering about the future just to validate your existence. Well, energy work like Reiki, Pellowah and Chi gung, to mention a few, belong to the group of the intangible, to the category of the Alternative medicine, and may get into your reality.

Alternative medicine, Traditional medicine, Eastern medicine, these categories are set behind the conventional medicine for in the later, it is the medical science which dominates.[47]

Alternative medicine evolves in a different category, in the emotional and spiritual realms, conventional medicine it's applied to the reality of the senses. Allopathic medicine deals directly with neuropeptides, proteins, chemical ligands,[48] enzymes, and all the bio-chemistry reactions residing in the human beings.

Data follow-up of treatments and Reiki sessions based on scientific observation is not yet considered a requirement to prove its effectiveness; Energy work practitioners have just relay on metaphysical theory, seeking to find answers in a conveniently and general abstract manner,[49] to help the public in general to create a context, so reason may grasp the concept of Reiki.

Energy medicine modalities are including principles of anatomy and physiology to explain how body postures, breath regulation, meditation, relaxation, and regulation of the mind may trigger bio-chemical reactions within the human body.[50]

Alternative medicine to play a condescending role within the conventional medicine, has included a functional medical treatment to its principles in a belief that this will improve the effects of a treatment, this new scientific trend is called Complementary medicine (CM) or Integrative medicine (IM).[51]

Studies have shown that energy work, or Chi kung, through inverted breathing, and placing the tongue on the root of the upper teeth can be used as vagal maneuvers; according to vagus nerve stimulation (VNS) therapy.[52] [53] where induced relaxation acts through the autonomic nervous system (ANS) to lower blood pressure and heart rate-regulated by the vagus or pneumogastric nerve, -the tenth cranial nerve- or CNX, to relieve tension and anxiety.[54]

Relaxation improves the properties of the immune system, also stimulating the brain's production of endorphins, which are natural opiates whose function is to decrease the perception of pain creating a state of well-being. [55] [56]

There are endless arguments against the performance of alternative medicine but consider the myriad of wellness programs those medical institutions today have adopted in their clinical practices to alleviate the severity of illness and physical pain, such as the hospitals mentioned above and their wellness programs developed in constant progress. Why? Because it has been proven that alternative medicine or holistic therapies can work to help patients cope with health problems, short and long term.

An interesting observation that I can include in this paragraph is that when I have offered a remote or face-to-face energy medicine intervention to a conventional medicine doctor, he has declined the offer, nodded his head in agreement or ignored it, even though we have known each other for a long time.

Distant or face to face energy interventions resonate when invoked being present on both, the conduit and the receiver may perceive manifested Vital Energy as a veil of breeze; or present as a magnetic field on the receiver, and as a quiet and still space on the sender, although the phenomenology may take different manifestations on each recipient of the energy medicine.

A Twisted Hop Within the Medical Area

During the weekly meetings attended by second level Reiki practitioners, students gathered to receive instruction from Master Jean C. Ferris of the Usui Shiki Ryoho System, based in El Paso, Texas. At that meeting, I shared my experiences related to Reiki energy work. I mentioned to everyone that during my visit to the dentist for an amalgam procedure, I had invoked the second level of Reiki empowerment. I combined the 1st (Cho Ku-Rei), and 2nd (Sei He Ki) symbols by drawing them in the air in front of me to "enhance" the anesthetics to exalt the noble purposes of the surgery, and thus avoid a painful experience while the surgery was taking place.

I began my story under the reassuring gaze of my companions waiting to hear it.

-Having invoked the first and second level Reiki symbols, I waited for the dentist to apply the injection of local anesthetic- I mentioned.

The dentist applied the second injection on another molar nerve to numb the area where he was going to work, and after two injections, the dentist left the operating room. After a few minutes, the assistant turned back to the room asking me if I could feel a strong cheek numbness. I told her that my cheek was not numb, which after a few touches to my gums and cheek with a dental instrument, she confirmed that the drug had not exerted an effect on me.

After waiting a few moments, the dental surgeon, after greeting me, checked the area to be operated on. He checked that the area was sensitive, he himself applied another cartridge of anesthesia on the two molar nerves to be numbed. A few minutes passed and the dentist asked me if my cheek was under the effects of the anesthesia, to which I answered in the negative. He checked the area and deemed it ready to perform the surgery. After the experience in the specialist's chair, I retired home surprised by the day's events.

I later discussed this medical issue with a 2nd. She tried to explain to me what she believed about this experience, but her answer did not fit with any of her experiences I have had with the Vital Force of the Reiki Energy.

49

Three months after, I met Lydia, in El Paso, she mentioned that she had visited the dentist, and after the doctor had applied an anesthetic on the gum, she had called the symbols to help her in this delicate situation. She wanted to be calmed and happy during the dental procedure.

With an inquisitive look in her eyes after Lydia had told the dentist's story, she asked me:

-And guess what Rene?

- I have not a clue- I responded.

-The anesthetic didn't work on me; the pain was unbearable.

Based in these facts, I did my research on questions pertaining the effects of the anesthesia such as, -is anesthesia, a high-risk medication? or was there a wrong moment to invoke the symbols because my body was weak and at risk on this situation? Are there are other high-risk medicines where the Reiki symbols may quash or modify its effects in the body?

I came up with interesting facts about the medication, which now I'll share with you.

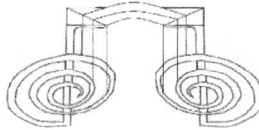

CHAPTER FIVE

SCIENCE VS. VITAL ENERGY

What happened here?

The presence of chemicals in the brain produces changes in the manifestations of the spirit as well as in the consciousness, thought and reasoning.[1]

The interference of the mescaline alkaloid found in the peyote plant, produces hallucinations and consciousness altered states, research has found out that the application of an anesthetic may bring people to lose them consciousness. In relation to anesthesia usages, Patricia Churchland's research mentions that, when visiting the dentist, the function of this medication is to 'freeze' the nerve of a molar, premolar, canine, or incisor, pushing the spirit to its edge to not feel pain in the tooth.[2]

Substances such as procaine -Novocain, according to brand name- supplied close to neurons that feed the tooth in question, 'disconnect' neuron responsiveness. This result inhibiting the pain signals sent to the brain because Novocain (procaine) is a local anesthetic aimed to cause loss of feeling (numbness) of skin and mucous membrane.

The way neurons enable and perform their normal function, is by the process of sodium ions hosted within the cell evicted outside its membrane so, when the neuron receives a stimulus, the channels regulated by voltage containing sodium are activated by entering the neuron, process called *action potential*. An action potential is an electrical signal that propagates along the membrane of a neuron or muscle fiber (cell); a rapid change in membrane potential that involves a depolarization followed by a repolarization.[3]

Because local anesthetics are drugs do block pain and other somatic sensations, the use of procaine and lidocaine temporarily block sodium transporters preventing neurons, to send a stimulus to the brain. Action potentials cannot propagate past the obstructed region, so pain signals do not reach the central nervous system.[4] After a while, the effect of procaine weakens allowing the dental nerve, gingiva, and cheek to recover its sensitivity, and after the neuron capacity stabilizes, then it recognizes the presence of pain.

Anesthesia's Toxicity

The systemic effects of local anesthetic toxicity can appear suddenly and acutely, within one to five minutes after being administered via muscle, with a range of 30 seconds to 60 minutes to manifest these symptoms.

Manifestations of systemic toxicity can be included in these areas:

- CNS -central nervous system-

- cardiovascular

- hematologic -*histologic, functional, and pathologic study of the blood*-

- allergic or

- local cellular tissue

Manifestations in the CNS

Systematic toxicity begins to manifest to excite the CNS, in the following way:

- Circumoral-around the mouth - or tongue numbness

- dizziness

- stunning

- black-out

- altered visual or auditory-difficulty focusing and ringing in the ears-tinnitus

- metallic taste

- disorientation

When it is administered in high doses, the disruption of the CNS can be followed by depression of the CNS with the following characteristics:

- Muscle spasms or muscle fasciculation

- coma

- respiratory depression and cardiac arrest

- convulsions

- loss of consciousness

- depression or cardiovascular collapse

- Cardiovascular signs

- Chest pain

- shortness of breath

- bewilderment

- palpitations

- hypotension

- diaphoresis-profuse sweating or

- fainting

Hematologic Manifestations

Frequent cases of *methemoglobinemia* have been reported in association with the use of benzocaine as an anesthetic. *Methemoglobinemia* is an abnormal blood condition in which a high level of methemoglobin, a type of hemoglobin, is produced. Hemoglobin is a protein that is produced in red blood cells, through which oxygen is transported throughout the body.

When *methemoglobinemia* occurs, hemoglobin is transported throughout the body, but is unable to be effectively received by the dermal tissue. Symptoms of acquired methemoglobin may include a bluish discoloration of the skin, headache, fatigue, shortness of breath or lack of energy.

In addition, *lidocaine*, also known as *xylocaine* and *lignocaine*, is mixed with small doses of epinephrine to be used to numb areas for lingering effects. When injected as a medication, it can begin to take effect in four minutes and last from half an hour to three hours.

Prilocaine has also been used for anesthetic purposes. Used in lower doses (1-3%), the methemoglobinemia can be asymptomatic, but supplied in large quantities (10-40%) can display the following symptoms:

- Cyanosis

- discoloration of the skin (gray)

- intolerance to exercise

- dizziness and syncope

- tachypnea

- weakness

- dyspnea dizziness

- fatigue

Allergic Manifestations

- Hives

- skin rash

- anaphylaxis---in rare cases—

According to the development of facts and the presentation of information about the effects of procaine, neurosurgical studies on neuronal functions and channels regulated by sodium voltage carriers, the "impending situation" of systemic toxicity of anesthesia can affect certain systems of the human body depending on the wrong prescription -and in other cases- by its proper use.

Depending on the symptoms and the result of the administration of an anesthetic, the invocation of Reiki, would act in favor of the universal energetic conduit keeping it safe from further and irreversible damage. With this in hand, it is justified that the wisdom of Reiki can intervene for a greater effectiveness of the local anesthetic, under the premise that its classification of substances includes a systemic toxicity -in my case, as explained above-.

Every event affecting the natural and flow balance in the universe, may be modified to its best resolution. We might agree in this case, the anesthesia didn't exert an inhibitory influence at a 100%, and as I recall there was pain, but not intolerable. There was pain, and could be worst, much worst that I would handle; so glad now, I wasn't forced to dash away from my seat.

Most Westerners process new information first on an intellectual level, and then apply this conceptual learning in a way that supports or invalidates the experiences based on the data collected. About the process for the mind to know, understand and learn new concepts there is a challenging scenario to open when talking about energy medicine. The part of the brain in charge of understanding new concepts first needs to relate the new information to similar ideas it has already processed.

If an attempt is made to place new abstract information in the brain that processes such concepts, the absolutes linked to energy work will show their effects in the physical world, the brain may become confused or inaccurately attempt to match this information with that already stored in the memory bank about a category of what might be Reiki or linear thinking. It will simply deny any information that might conflict with the physical body superimposed on the spiritual mind.

To deal with this existential predicament we make use of metaphors, analogies, absolutes about the existence of the cosmic energy, the Universe, God, Santa Claus, Life Force or Unconditional Love amongst some other infinites.

If you develop a philosophical approach to link the physical body with the spiritual, connecting both through emotions and psychological validations, such communion will become part in a new reality, a belief about your surroundings, your inner self, and about your faith.

> You know that the ground under your feet will not collapse, it won't disappear; this is your faith.

A belief is a concept that is not easy to explain because it is embedded within yourself, as polarities, it is in your beliefs, your fears, your environment, it is linked to those you love and hate, threaded by your daily habits and validated with a purpose about an expected destiny and your death.

The conception of Reiki was based on the work of an honest and spiritual man like Mikao Usui. His heritage is closer to our time so, it is not too much covered with emotional history. Without the bloodshed, religious confrontation, and the pursuit of greedy political power. Usui provided a shortcut that works very well. All it takes is the willingness to receive attunements from an authorized Reiki Master to begin activating the life force.

It is amazing how the invocation of the Reiki symbols can alter your reality, as I have seen this after invoking the symbols in many situations, each time; the Reiki energy will find a way to fix the underlying situation and the one that was invoked to help others. It will provide different alternatives that may not be immediately understood, but after a while the Life Force will reveal the mystery of your situation and bring you to an understanding of such a request.

Reiki embraces all types of situations like the financial, psychological, spiritual, emotional, and human relationships, but in the medical area, Reiki practitioners should be very careful because them are not physicians or certified counselors. The medical field is another branch in which everybody appeals to reach for healing purposes. Only medical doctors can heal; Reiki practitioners balance energies, provide relaxation sessions with positive results, and offer wellness benefits.

Medical doctors use another type of knowledge, as another type of magic translated from the shamans, wizards, and metaphysical sages.

Here is where the watershed highlights Faith Healing and Chemical Healing.

The revelation of the human body started as examinations of sacrificial victims evolving to the sophisticated analyses of the human body performed by the modern scientists. The study of human anatomy can be traced to the Egyptians, thousands of years before, but not as we know it today.

The development of the study of anatomy was gradually built upon concepts understood during the time of Galen, a physician, surgeon, and philosopher in the Roman Empire which slowly became a part of the traditional medical curriculum.[5]

Human anatomy has been characterized over time, by a continually developing understanding of the functions of organs and structures in the body.[6]

The winds of revelation were twining a new paradigm on how the scientific world worked around us.[7]

William Harvey, physician; Galileo Galilei physicist; Rene Descartes, and Francis Bacon, philosopher, and politician;[8] were trying to understand the questions which could reveal them why the blood is in constant motion? How to develop a systematic approach to physical phenomena observed in the heavens and on earth? How does behavior, brain, and mind work?[9]

And how to get to a materialistic and logical explanation for physical phenomena with a measured scientific method?

Medical knowledge improved before the Industrial Revolution with the participation of Rene Descartes. In the XVI century, the medical guild saw science in a different way, because of Descartes, a philosopher, mathematician, metaphysician, physiologist, and founding father of modern medicine.

Descartes made an explicit proposal in the 1640s by describing a model of how physical interactions in the material world could give rise to similar behaviors in humans.[10] Drawing on his unique knowledge of mathematics, Descartes proposed that phenomena as complex as human behavior could be seen as the product of purely physical interactions in physiological systems.[11]

Healing by faith involves a complex branch of emotions, and emotions have with recently technological innovations shown how these affect our health. Research has shown that the molecules of emotions which run in every system of the human body are linked to body-mind intelligence.[12]

So, from this perspective we can tell that body and spirit are closely related. However, before Descartes, the spirit was closely linked to emotions, and after his dissection practices he comes to join with the studies by William Harvey, Galileo Galilei physicist, and Francis

Bacon, and from this moment on, the minds of people were influenced in spirit and mind, that emotions had nothing to do with physical ailments.

Chemical Healing may involve the prescription of medication to balance the biochemical component of the body; medication to stir up the molecules of emotion.

The molecules of emotion, according to researcher Candice B. Pert, are found in the surface of body and brain cells functioning as the opiate receptor. Receptors work as sensors and scanners of external data, like our senses, but at a molecular level.

Because receptors are protein based, they cluster in the cellular membrane waiting for the right chemical key called *ligands*, allowing them to pass through the cellular membrane swimming in the extracellular fluid to bind.[13]

Circuit diagrams anatomists had been working for years, show neurological maps of peptides and their receptors. Such maps form a wiring connection in the brain showing an electrical reality by marking communication paths between the nerves, axons, and dendrites.[14]

The binding process is very selective. Ligands, which are smaller than receptors, bind by entering like a foot into a shoe, creating a molecular reaction to rearrange themselves, change their shape, connect the information that resonates to a certain situation.

Opiate receptors for instance can receive only ligands that are members of the opiate group like endorphins, morphine, or heroin. The receptor having received the information, sends it from the surface of the cell to a deeper level, where the cell shows a dramatic change, forming a biochemical chain reaction because of a message received by another cell, and starting from this reaction, a number of activities start to build up, like manufacturing new proteins, provoking decisions for cell division, opening or closing ion channels, or subtracting energy chemical groups shaking in this process the emotions, altering the mental, the spiritual, and the physical bodies.

There are three types of chemical ligands:

1. Neurotransmitters are small molecules made in the brain which carry information across synapsis between one neuron and the next. Acetylcholine, norepinephrine, dopamine, histamine, glycine, serotonin, and GABA, are types of neurotransmitters.[15]

The brain uses neurotransmitters to make the heartbeat, your lungs to breathe, and your stomach to follow the process of digestion. Neurotransmitters can also affect mood, sleep, concentration, weight, and can cause adverse symptoms when they are out of balance.[16]

2. Steroids is another type of ligands and include sex hormones - testosterone, progesterone, and estrogen. Steroids start out as cholesterol, which change its molecular structure into a specific kind of hormone. Enzymes in the gonads - testes and ovaries- change the cholesterol into sex hormone; other enzymes convert cholesterol into other kinds of steroid hormones, like cortisol, which under stress are secreted by the outer layer of the adrenal glands.

3. Peptides. These chemicals regulate practically all life processes are what Dr. Pert call as the molecules of emotion.[17]

Acetylcholine is made by the nerves, and it slows down the heartbeat and a rhythmic stimulation of the digestive system after eating, contributing both systems the digestive and the circulatory to a feeling of relaxation. Scientists theorized from such observations, that there were "site receptors," some in the heart muscles others on the digestive tract muscles, and still others on voluntary skeletal muscle, but have not demonstrated its existence.[18]

On site receptors Candice B. Pert Ph.D.,[19] has done a thorough study on the molecules of emotion, stating that emotions are the manifestation of neuropeptides created in the brain and other body sites. According to Pert, moods are modified by peptides which are proteins and recognized as the first life components, which make us the way we are, the way we think, feel, and perceive the world around us. A peptide consists of a string of amino acids, each joint together like a walking line of ants. Carbon and nitrogen are the bond that holds amino acids together. There are approximately 100 amino acids in the chain here, the peptide is a polypeptide, if there are more than 200 amino acids, it is called a protein.

Research found that peptides have existed in all parts of the brain,[20] not only in the hypothalamus, where endocrinologists thought traditionally were confined. Peptides also were found in a concentrated form at the cortex, the part of the brain where higher functions are controlled; also found in the limbic system, considered the emotional brain.[21]

By understanding the distribution of the neuropeptides through the nervous system, scientists found the lead to come up with a theory about these chemicals being the molecules of emotion.[22]

Reiki Scope Goes Beyond All Paradigms

Most people although feeling balanced and healthy don't know about the miracle processes held within themselves performed by the body cells, proteins, or biochemical elements to accomplish homeostasis. A person is not aware because is not attuned to the activity of these microscopic organic elements.

Peptides, receptors, and cells with different functions and organization roles within the eleven-human system, do not make the existence of the biophysical phenomena by manifesting a constant activity, and reporting to the human senses what it's going on to keep an inner balance through homeostasis. This would be too much for the brain to report to the human mind; it would be like showing data of the activity of these microscopic elements integrating the human body. Imagine passing all this data through a computer screen like a loop showing the same information repeatedly from birth to death, the information would be infinite with an endless number of pages, useless for the emotional mind and "less crucial to the smooth functioning of the body."[23]

Our inability to explain the biochemical processes of the human body does not invalidate the research that the medical profession has done today regarding their findings, but such a statement can be compared to a limited semantic record as the main tool to express to others how the flow of radiant medicine works throughout the body, and how this vital force of energy resonates through the human senses after having tried a Reiki session.

A simple explanation of what has been described in the previous paragraph would be better expressed with few pure absolutes. All cultures in the world best describe scientific findings, as well as philosophical and religious dogma with the use of absolutes. Absolutes-followed by mathematical formulas or citations from other scientists or philosophers, draw a better picture of the concepts we want to describe. A concept as an absolute, -such as *Heaven*- is drawn on a bigger space, so any individual no matter its background, can understand the essence of the concept based on the semantic[24] value attached to it.

Pure abstracts-such as Heaven-better identify a message by their cultural charge than a *dissecting set of abstracts* such as: *any of the places in the firmament or beyond the universe conceived of as domains of divine beings in various religions.*[25] To identify an experience, an explanation or a novel idea, as pure abstracts contain cultural keywords that clearly refer to a set of abstracts, rather than a dissection of abstracts, as this would be a bunch of clues to understand the sender's message, once the semantic filters are isolated.[26] Aristotle speaks of the representation of an abstract[27] in three ways:

The object -The symbol being represented.
The manner -The way the symbol is represented.
The means -The material that is used to represent it.[28]

The use of drawings, symbols, metaphors, hymns, logos, maps, graphs, flags, or a coat of arms, may be used to better understand abstracts, based on the concept that drawings may also represent compound words. "Tools as images, texts, and speeches are used by people to represent their reality, there is no direct approach -through the senses-[29] to understand reality."[30]

If religious matters are strong enough within your being, and your faith in spiritual beliefs is part of a reality that has been compiled through the practice of serious disciplines throughout your life, so the stoic side of your brain could accept this as an extension of the culture and religious faith of your ancestors, then the ritual and powers granted to your spirit will "effectively" transmit a beautiful and strong spiritual energy to others and yourself.

The above statements are very valid reasons to share and accept the absolute compassion and love of Reiki by believers from other spiritual energy fields, even from the scientific field as well, who have embraced the effective results and blessings of Reiki's healing power.[31]

There is no logical explanation as to how the power of Reiki works on people, animals, real time, or past and future situations, but Reiki will be present in a situation if you agree to receive it.

Reiki's life force comes from the highest realms of the vibrational essence. It doesn't pass through any logical, religious or imagery intentions. Reiki's force comes to the initiate as the form of an empowerment, a blessing. Blessings have no logical roots, there's no beginning for the unfolding of thoughts or causes. There are no steps to get the best outcome when relaying on a Reiki session; just like when observing the steps on a food recipe or when following the shortest route on a road map. Reiki manifests through the outcome of an unknown purpose of the universe, granted to the individual with unique and special qualities, as if them were an empty base to be filled up, this because the recipient's time has come to face a new energy medicine experience. The recipient's need to fill an empty spot in them soul, the search for truth, for balance, and joy has come to an end; the time has come for the *void* to be filled up with its own essence. There will be a peculiar way to be manifested because intrinsic vastness has born to be comforted; because new ways of thinking have demanded to be treated in a different way, for humanity has come to face other experiences and realities; from new ways for faith to be represented and by keeping away deviant meanings of manipulated selfish third-party's interests.

These statements may appear like wishful dreams, but absolutes tend to provide this impression. It may sound like cacophony language to the stoic mind, to the scientific mind which is used to follow a historic trend about cause and effect, a peculiarity of reason and lineal thought. Which statement is valid to justify the means of polarity and start the debate of scientific spirituality? The scientific method is a proof of gathered data base on a repeated cycle of cause and effect now, science may have its most ambitious challenge to set an analysis about energy medicine. Contemporary science has been along the orbits of new solar systems, around black holes, inside the physiology of viruses, and around the identification of emotions trough neuropeptides,[32] now energy medicine is its new goal, its new adventure, its new promise to humanity.

I wish for the scientific world to be interested in searching for these universal concerns, I want to know how the scientific method would be applied to unfold the mysteries of the sacred energies, for I am also part of this sequence of knowledge; I also believe in science.

No one before Dr. Usui made use of the healing field in the way Dr. Usui taught the first recipients. Takata's intervention and presence in Hayashi's life provided the right formula for the public exposure of Reiki to be effective in the western world.

Data can be found about other healers or prophets, who may have used Reiki as a means of healing before Dr. Usui, because other healing systems come from other branches, but from the same source, which is the higher unmanifested vibratory essence.

The effects of a Reiki session and its other modalities, always have a very profound effect on the spirit of the people who decide to experience a flow of energy. However, it is pure energy, because the human organism is composed of cells which in turn are made up of atoms. Quantum science has formulated theories and tested most of them, from which the results have corroborated the principles of the universe.

The human body is a miracle, it can reveal secrets of complex nature as it contains all the mineral and electromagnetic elements within its anatomical, physiological, and cellular structure.

Terrible battles can occur at the microscopic level between phagocytes and undesirable microbes that endanger the immune system. New cells regenerate entire tissues, following programs developed in their cellular memory over centuries. Their existence is a fact of life because with the nutrients at their disposal, the necessary water and oxygen, life will always be present and will adapt to the environment to survive and prevail in the animal kingdom.

The survival and adaptation program are not a set of recent autonomous programs, but have been adapting and evolving for centuries, because the basic elements necessary to prevail have the same code in the DNA.

The functions they perform as a complete system are always the same. The process of fertilization, the development of the eleven systems of the human body inside and outside the mother's womb, the trauma of birth, the first babbling and the precision of the first steps are the beginning of a long chain of achievements and functions performed by the human body.

The eleven systems of the body perform the same functions day after day, until they exhaust their energies to the point of fatigue and death.

Organs such as the stomach, lungs, heart, etc., work in unison and in complex harmony. They always perform the same functions. These are not new processes for the scientific mind, they have been repeating the same functions for years, lustrums, decades, and centuries. And this is where the medical profession has taken control of the situation.

It has discovered that the systems of the human body repeat the same functions to achieve its existence and that the alterations of its functions are due to external elements such as food, the quality of the air consumed, the elements that make up the water, the supply of medicines, the emotions that alter the balance of its functions when saturated with new information from the environment.

Medical science has invested efforts and much, much time to understand the complex order of the internal processes of the human body and its reaction to the elements of the environment.

The medical profession knows that the heart, for example, has repeated the processes for its existence for centuries, and will hardly change if this complex mechanism of its functions continues. It has little interest in the fact that the process of digestion is carried out by means other than the consumption and elimination of food through the digestive tract. The spiritual realm believes that the human body can acquire its energy sources through the consumption of nutrients from sunlight, or that subsistence nutrition could be limited to the small consumption of special herbs and in limited quantities.

The background comes from the practice of spiritual work and alternative medicine, which believes that universal energy can reverse the harmful effects of invading elements that have disproportionately altered the biological order of the human body and at the same time, altered its emotional, psychological, and spiritual functioning.

It is much easier for the logical mind to understand survival procedures than procedures to reverse the adverse elements of survival. The three logics of the brain work more easily with the reality of daily routine.

Limbic logic decides which option is best, safety or survival, and the options in the face of danger are fight, run or freeze.

Linear logic focuses on problem solving and decision making. The reasoning area is located mainly in the left hemisphere cortex of the brain.

Kinesthetic logic focuses on pleasure or pain, and its strength is in decision making. It considers immediate physical sensations, such as sounds, smells, pleasant images, tastes, and everything it touches, as most important.

Getting up, bathing, eating breakfast, going to work, attending to a concert, go to a bar, coming home for dinner and talk to family, and then going back to sleep so the next day you may go back to the same routine. It is much easier to live a normal life. Much easier for the logic of the brain.

The involvement in other activities, as an alternative to change daily routines, is an idea that in the long run, if not done consistently, will end up revealing in the person an illusory quality of existence, like the one witnessed in books or in the electronic media, ending up in the end in an unnecessary and useless effort. It is easier to devote oneself to familiar routines, if that ensures an easy and, at the same time, happy survival.

Of this the medical profession is completely sure, it is easier to continue the road already traveled than to initiate new paths, it is easier to repeat the same routines than to initiate others that are difficult and unknown. It is very likely that the scientific world will come to think about it:

'To complicate things includes too much risk, it is better to continue with what is established, and what has prevailed for centuries: the existential functions of the eleven systems of the human body.'

The Tangling of Energy Fields

The spread of Reiki has resulted in many sincere practitioners transcending spiritual levels, adding to these already existing symbolic labels in synchrony with other fields, and then sharing them with the technique to activate them.

The tangle of fields, added to Usui's initial cornerstone, is exposed to the thoroughness and complexity of the energetic fields, much like the complexity of the teachings of Buddha, Christ, Hermes Trismegistus, King Solomon, Don Juan, Einstein, and thousands of sincere practitioners before the spiritual mind.

Today there are a great number and variety of systems, methods, or schools of Reiki. All are valid if applied with unconditional love, knowledge, and responsibility. The energy comes from the same source, which is the Universe, from the same source within your mind.

The new Reiki modalities have emerged from certain processes of self-transformation, such as the case of Master Kathleen Ann Milner's Tera Mai Reiki, who included Tibetan and Buddhist symbols, already existing in the void, but discovered and activated by her. Kathleen Milner shares her findings on around 30 symbols, most of these shared by her students.[33]

The creation of *fields* as Reiki symbols is still growing, where every teacher starting a new discipline will feel touched by the power of the Universal Life Force, as a divine message because it adds new ideas and spiritual inspirations to understand different Reiki's ways of expression, having changed over the years while branching from the traditional Usui system.

The ways of transmitting communication vary from master to master, so each act as a conduit sharing their fundamentals in most cases of instruction and exchanging their content in some other situations. Many Reiki Masters have initiated students into the first, second and third levels of Reiki without the desire to enrich themselves but opening the doors to share such knowledge for free.

The confusion in the delivery of the teaching -compared to Usui's traditional scope- begins when the teachers have not been formally instructed in Usui's traditional system, and in the process of transitional initiations in the 1st, 2nd, or 3rd degree of Reiki.

New instructors come to eliminate or add new elements of symbols or initiations. This point is the creation of other forms of Reiki with surprising effectiveness.

I mentioned before, that for the field created to be effective, it must relate to other existing fields. There are no wrong fields, only different fields for very different but equally powerful purposes. Every vital energy practitioner will have to work at creating this field to discover and become accustomed to its potential.

So, in the end, this conjecture leads us to a central question, why are there so many modalities of Reiki? Why is the basic and advanced initiation not enough of this modality? Did Master Usui's teachings lack something that his followers of the independent guild - the third branch - of Reiki were able to see?

Does the universal energy continue to provide talents to all who have known the divine breath? Perhaps a spiritual rebellion has been unleashed in which everyone claims to be the possessor of true spiritual liberation.

Is it possible that at the end of this enlightened age there will be thousands of sacred symbols bestowed upon each new adept initiated through the divine breath of life, after their initiation?

Do some Reiki practitioners consider that something is missing in Mikao Usui's original Reiki system, so they should ask other masters to correct, complete or strengthen the unlinked fields?

Did the original descendants of the Usui master intentionally -or accidentally- omit to create in this way, independently, another form of "Reiki", which would not be a descendant of the Usui Reiki lineage, but another modality of Reiki, thus initiating another field linked to the original Usui Reiki field? Was Dr. Usui's way of healing different from Dr. Hayashi's or Takata's?

Maybe they are hidden, the different names attached to the root of Reiki.

Discharge of other Vital Energy Modalities

The traditional method of Usui Reiki, taught by Hawayo Takata, was modified, and adapted to the needs of the West, thus achieving its full acceptance. The alterations and omissions that were made to the methods and history of Reiki were essential at the time, thus achieving its accreditation and diffusion worldwide. Usui's traditional Reiki is the seed that gives origin to other Reiki methods.

Another Reiki modality is Karuna Reiki, synthesized by William Lee Rand after the discovery of the new symbols of other Reiki Masters, which "activate more specific energies".

Karuna is a Sanskrit word used in Hinduism and Buddhism. In the Reiki Ho style, there are original techniques and positions as taught by Mikao Usui. The Seven Degree Reiki energetic modality is a method developed by Master Barbara Weber Ray. This method consists of seven levels corresponding to each of the seven chakras. Barbara Ray through various initiations "activates different sources of energy, complemented with different practices."

Master Ishikuro developed Raku Kei Reiki Iris, a student of Master Takata, who along with Arthur Robertson, is the founder of the American Association of Reiki Masters.

According to Robertson, Raku means vertical energy and Kei means horizontal energy that flows through the body. Raku is known as "The Way of the Fire Dragon" and is the science of spiritual overcoming based on the ancient teachings of Tibet. It is the method taught by Takata with the addition of master frequency generators, originally created by Rolf Jensen and white light calligraphy, added by Ishikuro.

It differs in the application of attunement, "giving rise to higher consciousness." This method works with three main channels that carry energy throughout the body, the Shushumna, Ida and Pingala. Rolf Jensen, a physician, went to Japan to study with Japanese doctors, who heard about Dr. Usui's work and, upon searching for detailed information about the Reiki system, discovered that the "master key that Usui used in his initiations has been lost."

In 1952, he found what he considered the "key", a symbol that conquered all diseases. After much work, he finally found the answer in a mixture of silver nitrate that combined the frequencies of the 7 primary colors and the sound of the seven (7) musical notes. The combination formed seven atomic seals found on planet Earth. The symbol was called: The Master Frequency Symbol.

> *Seekers can create and potentiate symbols, mantras and spells based on the strength of the complexity of the superstring within the fields pursued to be activated through the shamanic method.*

The effectiveness of Reiki modalities depends on how practitioners use the sacred symbols received during initiations and the skills developed as conduits of vital energy and understanding of the symbol's attribute.

If so, we are living an impressive and wonderful spiritual revolution that even the scientific community has been attracted by such a unique similarity between spirituality, quantum fields and the biochemistry of the human body, especially regarding superstrings, neuropeptides and the effects that physical contact can produce.

The *Crown ReiQi©* Master Modality

The hand positions indicated in the *Crown ReiQi,©* book are not simply random positions to give significance to this modality.

Each hand position contains a complex mechanism of energy flow that is achieved through visualization.

Each position invokes images of power that precede it, plus all positions are empowered by the invocation of the Reiki symbols of the second level of Traditional Usui Reiki.

In my workshops, 1st and 2nd level Reiki practitioners are empowered with the potentialities of this new modality called *Crown ReiQi©* Supersymmetry, at the master level.

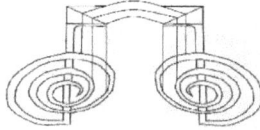

CHAPTER SIX

THE HISTORY BEHIND ITS ORIGIN

The Order of the Factors Does Not Alter the Product

This principle may not have universal applications as would be the case with following a cooking recipe to the letter, or the process for successfully performing open-heart surgery, etc. But in the case of accumulating the potential to go through life with a positive attitude that everything one does is backed by a structured plan, the principle that the order of factors does not alter the product is well applied.

Within spiritual practices, whatever one does, the result of the intention should always be structured with positive feelings and actions.

An action of a positive nature will always generate a positive result. A positive action accumulates in a database, just as a dollar saved will remain in a savings bank.

Generous actions accumulate in the human body like a database. These actions end up manifesting in the behavior of the person with an attitude of service. A behavior that becomes the destiny of a person with awakened consciousness, and by awakened consciousness I mean every person who thinks about the welfare of his fellow man, about personal self-development, about the awakening of the balance of the physical, mental, emotional, and spiritual bodies, about the consciousness of creating a better world for humanity. A person who acts in this way lives his destiny with love and dignity, a destiny traced by a noble and focused character, based on analogous habits and customs, and positioned in the memory based on action.

All action is based on words, on words to provoke action, on words that were created by the essence of thoughts.

These qualities may seem difficult to carry out at this time, but I have met thousands of people who have developed in their lives, an altruistic vision, and a concern for their fellow man.

Actions done for the benefit of others are created fields that constantly vibrate and have the power to resonate with other nuclei of a similar nature.

In the trajectory of my life, there have been adversities and good opportunities to take advantage of both. Adversities made me stronger as I had to avoid them to stay out of trouble, I saw how some of my peers had fun doing mischief to other people; actions that I did not dare to imitate. I saw that they enjoyed doing it and I was left behind in this fun, but how I enjoyed it after they were punished for what they had done.

I don't want to say that I was a prude, for I also did two or three pranks, but I outsmarted my classmates; I didn't get caught. In the end I paid the consequences of those pranks, so I learned that he who does it, pays for it. I became aware of these mistakes and focused on just being a better individual. I concentrated on spiritual, mystical, and self-improvement studies. The search for spiritual instruction opened several doors for me, which continue to open to this day, among which I will mention the following.

The light of life gave me the opportunity to be a member of the Rosicrucians; to belong to Master Andrew Da'Passano's esoteric transcendental meditation group; to be a student and practitioner of Chi kung, taught by the Taoist priests of the San Francisco Martial and

Medical Arts Sanctuary in San Francisco, Cal. Dali lama while receiving Medicine Buddha, Green Tara and White Tara attunements, along with thousands of others in San Diego, California; I was initiated as a teacher/practitioner of the Usui Shiki Ryoho Reiki modality and received initiations as a practitioner of the Pellowah energetic modality.

I attended other courses, workshops, sessions, talks and energy exchanges of other spiritual modalities.

These fields of knowledge have the attribute that they all explore positive energetic fields, a vibration of the higher spiritual spheres. I have not been interested in exploring the lower vibrational energies, which I am exposed to daily when I go to the mall, pick up the new license plate for my car or attend a social event. Although I do not seek out low vibrational energies, they appear along with the positive energies.

The energies always come in pairs: Yin and Yang, black and white, positive, and negative, etc., none of them alone will bring about the liberation of consciousness, but the polarity that one chooses is the one that can best lead us to fulfill our mission in life.

The search for my inner self always bore fruit, and in every session or workshop I attended, I always felt the presence of something greater than myself, something that I cannot describe in words, but the presence of that something always showed itself when invoked or when I felt a higher presence. In every exercise or meditation, I did, I was always answered, and the doors were always open to me, every day.

Sometimes life seems like a beast trying to devour us.

We only remember the negative experiences and the positive ones remain hidden in certain areas of the brain. When we are children, we perceive happy moments and sad events. However, we forget the pleasant moments, such as the fun times with our elementary school friends, the times our mother cooked for us, the celebration of our first birthdays. Usually, these memories stay in the background, while the unpleasant moments remain vivid in the memory. They make us feel that we are not smart enough to excel in school, that we don't get what we want, or that we don't feel completely loved. Sometimes we look for ways to get attention to gain acceptance, to no avail.

Mark Wolin, in his book *It Didn't Start with You*, mentions that when we are children, we experience that our safety and well-being are threatened by events in our environment, so our body reacts by looking for ways to defend itself. These unconscious defenses become a pattern of reacting to what we find difficult or disturbing, rather than focusing on what would give us inner peace of mind.

This background is supported by evolutionary biologists. Scientists describe how the amygdala uses two-thirds of the neural network to detect intimidating situations. Because of this identification process, painful and traumatic events remain stored in long-term memory, in contrast to pleasant events. From these observations, he emphasizes that the defense mechanism is mainly based on the imminent attack mechanism.[1]

Life itself has its ups and downs. If you are presented with ups and downs, apply the belief that this is a positive action, so that the mind develops plasticity in the brain as a progressive experience; if you are presented with downs, recognize them as a life lesson, so that your mind positions them in positive memories.

This thinking mechanism will allow you to de-power a negative experience, giving you the power of a life lesson, which will prevent you from making the same mistake twice, and if you don't learn not to make the mistake twice, a third chance will come.

But to believe that thinking only happy thoughts will solve the barriers of adversity is not entirely realistic. Trying to change the behaviors that keep us in a frame of perception of hopelessness, in the face of our expectations of a life free of worries and problems, requires much more than rationalizing our situation.

To see any change in your life, you must engage in activities that will change the quality of your life. You must embody[2] the change that will lead you to a new perception of your role as an achiever, and to get there, you must physically engage in activities that lead you to act.

To see a change in the events of your life, action is the key, and if it is accompanied by a visualization mechanism, the results will be promising.

Visualization alone will not give the expected results, but strengthened by action, the expectation that you will get what will bring you great benefits, will be behind the door. All you must do is open it, considering what suits you best: victorious moments or bitter tasting experiences.

The practice of the *Crown ReiQi©* modality, when performed with these points in mind: a positive attitude, with the body and face relaxed and with a smile, will be embodying a level of perception on a conscious and subconscious level. Here, the action of touching the hands and face together with the perception of what is being felt, will create a space to generate a change in behavior.

This polarity of thought pattern will strengthen you over time: practice and awareness of events. The fighting habit will awaken in you the quality of a warrior, a quality that has been dormant deep in your psyche for a long time.

Because you are a warrior, a fighter. I will explain.

Before you were born, you proved yourself to be a great strategist and a tough opponent to beat. You faced millions, approximately 200 to 300 million opponents. You saved your life, causing the rest to fail in their mission. You were victorious and managed to awaken to life. The spark of life within you, gave you a physical body to carry out a life purpose, given to you to discover other worlds. It is in this life that you must work internally to achieve your life purpose. Why did you come to this world? What is your mission? are some of the many questions you must answer.

The fact that you have a physical body gives you the right to achieve whatever goals you set for yourself in life. You just must work internally to remember that you are a winner, a warrior.

You as well as millions of other warriors share the same world, you will only have to work with them in harmony, where you will have to develop new strategies to increase your inner power.

Crown ReiQi© is a great tool to develop this power, you only need to create the habit of practicing certain exercises that will attune you to high vibrational fields, and if you have practiced inner balance through service to others during your life, you will be very close to multiplying the results that result from your practices.

But this is not the end of your role as a winner. In your mother's womb, you were in contact with the void of creation. During the nine months of gestation, your organism developed eleven systems to perfection, which served as tools to adapt to an unknown world. These eleven systems are:

Circulatory System / Cardiovascular System, Digestive System and Excretory System, Endocrine System, Integumentary System / Exocrine System, Muscular System, Nervous System, Renal System / Urinary System Reproductive System, Respiratory System, and the Skeletal System.

From the moment of fertilization, you were always protected by a superior being, who no one dared to interfere in his mission of protector, and unconditional provider of special nutrients for your development. This exceptional being, unique in the world, served as your guardian to keep you safe even at the cost of her life (which is your mother).

Then you entered a new universe, that of cause and effect. You experienced the creation of life from emptiness, from a void escorted by tranquility, by the security provided by a space where the manifestation of life is gestated. From an absolute emptiness, which preserves the secret of manifestation, hidden until it is invoked in every intention to create things in the world of the third dimension. You were born from a watery world, from a silent world without light, assimilating the experience of millions of cells that form your body. You did not know what the future held for you, until the door of light opened, the door of birth, the opportunity to have a life, and so you were born, like a miracle.

From that moment on, your parents take care of you, they breastfeed you, they cover you when you are cold, they lull you to sleep, they give you medical care and above all they give you protection and love.

They protect you because for them, you are the best thing that could have happened in their lives.

You are a miracle, make your life the best and most positive experience. You have the formula in your DNA, this formula knows how to do it.

The History Behind Its Origin

People form their character throughout their lives with varied experiences through daily interaction with other people, experiences arising from courses taken in educational institutions, whether in public classrooms, in front of a tele-information course, or through family and friends' meetings.

The tools for understanding your reality may vary, such as the scenarios that served for the interpretation of perceptions about the environment, the exercise of moral norms, or existential beliefs coming from your culture or the mass media, as well as the way of decoding the information received by the senses of hearing, touch, sight, smell, and taste.

Each person's behavior functions as a program, imprinted by perceptual signals from the senses and information stored in the brain, useful for playing a role that positions him or her in an environment according to his or her qualifications. Interactions can take place in different environments, and the decision to participate in any field is a very individual decision.

In the field of spiritual sciences, there are many options from which people can choose according to their interests of inner advancement and their economic possibilities.

The energetic modalities that I was able to explore, most of them came to me by synchronicity. Each energy line that I was able to understand came to me, without knowing for sure what this modality would bring to my spiritual advancement. I gladly adopted them as my own and the results were extraordinary.

Over the years I practiced many fascinating spiritual disciplines and to this day the seeds planted continue to multiply abundant blessings.

I have no distinction between exceptional events and discouraging events or experiences, for me everything enters the scale of values that will enrich my existential experience. I submit all experiences to the law of polarities, and of cause and effect, knowing that each one of them appears, and then after manifesting itself, it polarizes to another emotion, and then it disappears. The process is presented in a cyclical way, like the existential polarities of human beings.

No matter the emotion to which we are exposed, negative or positive, the gain will always be 100%, because even when we are living a bad moment, the experience will be 100% gain, because we are alive.

This possibility of being alive is what makes us warriors, achievers. We have the power to overcome any adversity that comes our way, no matter how difficult it may seem. Life is the solution, because it is always in constant development, if there is life there is abundance.

With this, I illustrate that when performing an action, another one with the same intensity is taking place, but in the opposite direction, but it doesn't matter which direction it may take, the result will be +100% because life resonates with light.

The perception of time and space is cyclical because the programming in which humanity evolves is cyclical. We are born to die, we inhale to exhale, we wake to sleep, we speak to be heard and listen to think, and so on.

The experiences that come from spiritual practice are often shrouded in a veil of mystery, a mystery that may not be clear, but which the student must weigh against the possibilities of pleasant or ambiguous experiences.

The origin of *Crown ReiQi©* began almost 40 years ago, the first manifestation of the modality was presented to me in 2017. Five years later, during a visit to Europe in 2022, other ways of understanding vital energy applied to health and inner balance were revealed to me.

In September 2017, while sleeping in my home in Phoenix, Arizona, I had a strange apparition. A force subtly forced me awake and upon opening my eyes, I saw across the room a gray, square-shaped cloud slowly moving toward the right side of the room, traveling in a linear trajectory. The shape had a cloudy condition. Its rhythm was slow and steady, and looking at this moving shape I could make out a square figure of approximately 12"x10". I observed this shape closely, and could tell that it had a skull shape, looking to the right and straight ahead.

The nebulous figure slowly advanced about four feet, and as I watched it move, immediately this "shape" felt the weight of my sight on it and began to move away from the wall taking an orbital trajectory towards where I was, towards the bed I was resting on. I saw this shape approaching and slowly moving towards me. My wife, who was sharing the bed, was still sleeping and I could even hear her rhythmic breathing. I didn't try to wake her up because I was paying attention to the "cloud" approaching me.

At that moment, all those movies about aliens and poltergeists went through my mind in fast motion; but ignoring this, I just concentrated on being mindful not to lose my temper as I watched this strange - or extraordinary - being approach me. I held on to stay calm. The cloud was getting closer and closer, and while processing the incident, I decided to send the second and the first Usui Traditional Reiki symbol -as a greeting or warning- to that entity. The form began to back away -perhaps surprised by my courage or by the power warnings I had sent it-, and moved to the right, near the threshold of the bathroom door, on the far right.

The skull shape continued to recede until it was hidden on the dark side of the door frame; I could barely make it out. The form remained in the same place for a long time, radiating a kind of vapor. The entity stared at me, but I stared back, not in defiance, but in expectation of what was about to happen next. After a few minutes, I continued to watch it until I got bored, falling asleep immediately.

The next morning, I woke up and realized that the cloudy figure had disappeared. I told my wife what had happened and both she and I were silent, amazed at what had happened the night before.

Incidents Vibrate within the Superstrings

My wife has a great interest in the study of higher cosmic beings.

Every year for the past three years, she has wanted to attend a conference sponsored by the Group of Forty[3] which this year was held in Prescott, AZ. My wife signed up for the event, called "Future Earth -Evolving to a 5th Dimensional Planet for Personal and Planetary Healing." The conference was scheduled for September 29-October 1, 2017.

Rocio, my wife, had been preparing for this event for three years, and was eager to enjoy presentations by experienced people such as author and multidimensional channel David K. Miller, to hear lectures by Gudrun R. Miller, a past life therapist and visionary artist. I was interested in hearing Dr. Heather and Dr. Michael Davis speak about Native American spiritual wisdom and methods to enhance the immune system by raising one's personal vibrational frequency.

On Friday at noon, my wife Rocio and I arrived in Prescott, AZ. at a beautiful resort, and then went directly to the conference room at 2:00 PM. to attend the introduction of the course.

The next day, at 8:30 a.m., the program organizers had already planned for the attendees to show up for the first lecture.

After attending the first talk, Rocio had the first ten-minute brake at around 10 a.m. and, after we gathered, she cheerfully mentioned that she had requested a chart reading for me with the astrologer, Elizabeth HeartStar.[4] The news took me by surprise, but within five seconds I felt a warm sensation inside.

Tucked into a corner, Elizabeth motioned for me to sit across from her, pointing to a chair with a wiggle of her nose as she greeted me cordially. I sat down as I watched Elizabeth contemplate a beautiful deck of cards on a beautifully carved wooden table. HeartStar, asked me to introduce myself and asked me a couple of basic questions, and after I answered, I told her about my experience with the presence of the silent skull. As I spoke of this incident, she looked at me with peculiar interest and asked me to wait in my chair -that she would be right back.

Elizabeth left her space to return to her seat after five minutes.

- Rene," said Elizabeth, "when I heard your story it crossed my mind that you had an encounter with a crystal skull.

- What? -asked my brain; Elizabeth understood my question by the look in my eyes.

- After having done an instant meditation, Elizabeth said, -I have received a message from the crystal skull; ...sometimes "she" tells me that she "wants" to be close to a person to give him a message, and "she" -the crystal skull-, wants to spend some time with this person. Rene, I will lend you the skull for a couple of hours, so you can contact "her". After saying this, he placed a straw basket on his lap and carefully took out a package, and unwrapping its contents, he showed me a medium sized crystal skull, and along with the skull he took out a rounded crystal quartz, to use as a base. She showed me both treasures and began to wrap each one with a special cloth placing both objects in a bag of soft material, and inside a handbag.

- Elizabeth, are you telling me you are going to lend me the crystal skull for a couple of hours? - I asked in amazement.

- Yes, two to three hours, you just must bring it back before five o'clock in the afternoon, which is the time when the lectures will end for the day.

I did not think her proposal far-fetched, nor did I question Elizabeth's suggestion that she had communicated with the crystal skull model, but condescending to what she had said, I took the basket for the purpose of finding a clue to what had happened that peculiar night when the figure appeared.

-Very well," I said, and taking the basket, I gratefully walked away. At that moment I felt very honored to take that mysterious object with me and meditate on Crystal's skull with the intention of receiving the message I was unable to receive the night "she" visited me.

I returned to the hotel room and began a series of meditations. After invoking the Reiki, I-II and III symbols, I opened my mind to whatever might occur. After a while with my eyes closed, I saw an image formed of three blue lines, I saw it once and concentrated on its shape, the image kept coming not once, but several times until I confirmed that I had seen it clearly. It was, without a doubt, a blue furcula. Other messages came to my awareness such as: how to meditate inside the crystal skull and its entry point to apply to certain areas of the brain in need of being restructured with vital energy. Remember that cells have memory and helping them to be, by cleansing them of toxins, traumas or energetic blockages will help them to reconnect with each other. The purpose of the *Crown ReiQi* manual technique is to create through repetition, the field existing in the void, but crystallized through practice, intention, conviction, and faith, which is the ultimate condition of our reality.

Elizabeth HeartStar hit the nail on the head with her finding about my story, and my quest to find out the purpose of the presence of the cloudy figure seemed to be about to be revealed, and with it the answer to get out of the uncertainty.

I researched in several books on symbols, to find out if the image of the furcula had been analyzed before; there was no information about it. One day, while practicing a directed energy exercise, I suddenly froze while observing the palms of my hands, there I saw the furcula embedded in the center of my palms. The three lines I saw while meditating with the crystal skull were in front of my eyes. The *line of head*, the *line of life* and the prolongation of the *line of head* going towards the dorsal edge of the hand.

During the following weeks, as I meditated, I asked my spirit guides about how to transfer attunements to others interested in the initiation of this modality. I asked many times for guidance, but the answers did not manifest so quickly, weeks went by, and when I least expected it, I got the answer on the method of passing the attunements to others. In two other books on the *Crown ReiQi©* modality, I explain the technique of how to receive attunements and the hand positions related to this vital energy modality.

In the second volume on the energetic modality: *Crown ReiQi©* as Energy Catalyst/Hands are Energy Tools, and in the third volume I explain the process of the empowerments in: *Crown ReiQi©*: Positioning Energetic Resonance. These three volumes were written so that the student can perform self-treatments and give treatments to others. There is another book, the master level book that comprises the information in the previous volumes and this one: The Energy and Science: The History behind Its Origin.

The master level book is called: *Corona ReiQi©*: Supersymmetry.

The Crystal Skulls

Today the *Crystal Skulls* discovered in the late 19th century have been the subject of ongoing mystery and controversy. According to people who claimed to have discovered close to a dozen carved skulls made of clear or milky white quartz, they date back thousands or even tens of thousands of years, from ancient Mesoamerican civilizations such as the Aztecs, Toltecs, Mixtec or Mayans.[5]

In 1924, British adventurer Frederick Mitchell-Hedges led an expedition to Lubaantun, an ancient Maya city deep in the Yucatan jungle in modern Belize, now considered an archaeological reserve, his adopted daughter Anna, found inside a Mayan pyramid,[6] one of the most mysterious objects in archaeology: a crystal skull created from a single solid piece of clear quartz. Since the discovery of the Mitchell-Hedges skull, as it is called, a story has been created about the origin of its supernatural powers and legendary civilizations.[7]

Recently, with the use of compound electron microscopes, scientists at the British Museum in London and the Smithsonian Museum of Natural History in Washington, D.C., performed analyses of glass skulls finding marks that could only have been made by modern carving implements - rather than the stone, bone and wooden tools that would have been used in pre-Columbian times - their conclusion was that the skulls were probably fakes and were manufactured in the late 1800s, in response to a surge of interest in the ancient world and its artifacts.[8]

Honoring Skull Celebration

Mexico celebrates the *Day of the Dead* with totem skeletons and skulls, where offerings are made to family ancestors. Also, intertwined in the roots of their faith, they worship a saint known as *Santa Muerte*, where believers claim she is very miraculous and protective of her followers.

Among Mesoamerican civilizations, there was a tradition of displaying skulls on a skull rack or 'tzomanti.' This was used for the public display of human skulls, typically those of war captives or other sacrificial victims.[9]

In Hinduism, the goddess of death, Kali, is often depicted with a garland of skulls. Kali has been worshipped by devotional movements and tantric sects as the Divine Mother, Mother of the Universe, Adi Shakti, or Adi Parashakti. Kālī is the feminine form of 'time' or 'the fullness of time' with the masculine noun 'kāla', —and by extension, time as the "changing aspect of nature that brings things to life or death."[10]

The Capela dos Ossos (Chapel of Bones) is one of the best-known monuments of Évora, Portugal. It is a small interior chapel located next to the entrance of the Church of San Francisco. The chapel gets its name because the interior walls are covered and decorated with human skulls and bones.[11]

I witnessed these human remains in the year 2022, there I felt the place charged with a kind of solemn energy, not dark or heavy, but being there was a way of disrespecting these remains. I did not try to penetrate their energetic bubble since it was not of my interest, but I perceived that death is always tied to life, and to understand this insight, it is not necessary to have spiritual knowledge, any layman or laywoman can understand it. It is perceived as a natural state of life.

A more positive way to show a symbolic side of the exhibition of thousands of skulls and skeletal bones are the remains of 3,700 bodies of Capuchin friars found in an ossuary in Rome; the *Capuchin Crypt*, a small space comprising several small chapels located under the church of Santa Maria della Concezione dei Cappuccini on Via Veneto near Piazza Barberini in Rome Italy.

This bizarre display of human remains, collected between 1528 and 1870, decorates the crypt walls in dramatic baroque and rococo style.[12] The Catholic order insists that the display is not meant to be macabre, but a silent reminder of the rapid passage of life on Earth and our own mortality.

Within the Mexican community the *Holy Death*, an intimidating skeletal figure holding a scythe, is venerated by many names, most notably *La Santa Muerte*. Although the worship of Santa Muerte/La Santa Muerte has become inextricably entangled with the drug cartels, it has become a deity for all working class and lower income Mexican citizens, not just criminals.[13]

Although *La Santa Muerte* has no clear roots, some believe that the popular saint emerged as a combination of Spanish Catholicism and the Aztec cult of Mictecacihuatl,[14] the Queen of the underworld and the afterlife. Nevertheless, believers recognize the *Santa Muerte* as their patron saint, and the number of devotees continues to grow, although the Catholic Church has not canonized or approved Santa Muerte or La Santa Muerte.

Human sacrifice was in this sense the highest level of a whole panoply of offerings through which the Aztecs sought to repay their debt to the gods. Aztec priests sacrificed war captives to Huitzilopochtli, a war deity, the sun, and the patron of the city of Tenochtitlan.[15] With the use of an obsidian blade or flint, the priest would cut the abdomen of sacrificial victims placed on a sacrificial stone, to reach the heart and be torn out, still beating it was held up to the sky in honor of the Sun-God.[16]

Although sacrificed prisoners of war and the skulls of other victims were considered war trophies, human hearts were also displayed to the public. Heart extractions and sacrifice were seen as a 'supreme religious expression' among the ancient Maya. It is believed that the extraction had multiple steps for preparation and proper respect for the gods.[17]

Catholic priests showed the Mesoamerican natives that these types of sacrifices were considered a sin and under the new religion, they were not accepted by God. The Franciscan priests taught the Mesoamerican natives new ways to show respect for the human body. Based on the religious practice of offering the victim's heart to the gods, the Catholic priests reminded the natives of the sacredness of the heart and the rest of the human body. The priests taught them about devotion to the Sacred Heart (also known as the Sacred Heart of Jesus, *Sacratissimum Cor Iesu* in Latin) which is one of the most widely practiced and well-known Catholic devotions, in which the heart of Jesus is seen as a symbol of "God's boundless and passionate love for humanity."[18] Also, greatly aiding the early missionaries was the image known as the Virgin of Guadalupe.[19] Beliefs and traditions modify societies where events over time become magical and embedded with special spiritual qualities. There is much information about events that are not shared with the masses but are kept secret or simply to be revealed to the chosen ones.

I have no particular interest in promoting the existence of the Crystal Skulls, but the vision I had of the skull in the middle of the night connected a message of other events related to its essential attributes. As mentioned earlier, its qualities come from a hidden dimension unknown to human beings, it comes from the higher noetic world, the world of ideas, causes and effects; from the *noumenon*.[20] Ideas, images and manifestations downloaded from the void and brought into the world of the third dimension, can be labeled by its creator with any name; even bestowing magical or spiritual characteristics upon it. People will strengthen their traits over time by practice, belief, and respect.

Sacredness of the Human Body

Although history has reported a hateful side of human nature in some cultures, there are other historical facts where human beings have shown deep respect for the human body. Science has been concerned with health care and service to the community other institutions such as the Red Cross, have emphasized altruism and care for the needy as their humanistic banner.

Throughout the centuries, mankind has considered the human body as the image and vehicle of divinity to be recognized as sacred and cherished as its refuge. Most cultures even consider the human body as a temple where they can meet and talk to God.

There is no doubt that the earliest cultures have respected and honored the human body, whether friend or foe, have shown their way to honor the sacredness of the human body in different ways. The justification of certain rituals or hateful customs practiced in the past will not be valid or admissible under the basic principles of love and respect for other living beings. It never has been and never will be.

The *Crown ReiQi*© modality is a practice used to help humanity, advance it energetically and scientifically, and put into practice the basic principles of anatomy and physiology. The exploration of the brain is opening new frontiers of science, and laymen can take advantage of new scientific discoveries to help balance their bodies. If body balance means health balance, this could also include mental, emotional, and spiritual balance. In depth, the *Crown ReiQi*© modality means holistic balance, which has been the purpose, and the mission to pursue, of all civilizations.

This volume has been written with the best intention of providing valuable information to the reader and awakening interest in learning a little more about this *Crown ReiQi*© modality. The results of the energetic sessions of this modality have been very well received and have been recommended by patients who have undergone the universal energetic experience. If your interest in beginning a serious study of this modality is not your preference, I invite you to discover how scientific advances increasingly resemble the knowledge of ancient energy balancing practices in the different cultures of the world, kept for centuries in their cultural archives, some public, others secret and sacred, only revealed to the initiated.

NOTES

Prologue

1. Brown, Fren, "Living Reiki, Takata's Teachings", no 3, 45-60, (1992).
2. Ibid
3. Usui, Mikao, Dr., Arjava, Petter, Frank, The Original Reiki Handbook of Dr. Mikao Usui, Lotus Press, Shangri-La, Twin Lakes, WI.,4th. Eng., Ed., 2003.
4. Ibid.

Introduction

1. https://www.sciencebuddies.org/science-fair-projects/science-fair/steps-of-the-scientific-method
2. https://en.wikipedia.org/wiki/Optogenetics
3. Kaku, Michio, The Future of the Mind, Pinguin Random House Group Editorial,2014.
4. https://plato.stanford.edu/entries/scientific-discovery/
5. https://www.healthline.com/health/top-10-deadliest-diseases#cad
6. https://www.medicalnewstoday.com/articles/308772.php#what-happens-in-a-reiki-session

Chapter One

1. https://www.brainhq.com/brain-resources/brain-plasticity/what-is-brain-plasticity
2. https://www.brainhq.com/brain-resources/brain-plasticity/brain-plasticity-exercises
3. Ibid.
4. Hudman, Andy, "Learning and Memory", no.1, 1-11, (2006)

Chapter Two

1. *www.reiki.org/reikinews/rn090199.html*
2. https://en.wikipedia.org/wiki/Mikao_Usui
3. Tortora, Gerard J., Derrickson, Bryan, "Principles of Anatomy and Physiology", no. 14, 495-545, (2009).
4. Ibid.
5. Ibid.
6. http://www.medicalnewstoday.com/articles/7624.php
7. Ibid.
8. Ibid.
9. Tortora, Gerard J., Derrickson, Bryan, "Principles of Anatomy and Physiology", no. 14, 495-545, (2009).
10. Ibid.
11. http://old.post-gazette.com/healthscience/20011023hreiki1.asp

Chapter Three

1. Ellyard, Lawrence, *Reiki Healer- A Complete Guide to the Path and Practice of Reiki*, Lotus Press, Twin Lakes, Wisconsin 53181, 2004.
2. http://www.reiki.org/FAQ/HistoryOfReiki.html
3. http://www.reikisystem.com
4. http://www.awakening-healing.com/Reiki.htm
5. http://mygaiany.com/2017/02/history-reiki-usui-reiki/
6. https://en.wikipedia.org/wiki/Mikao_Usui
7. http://www.reiki.org/FAQ/MrsTakataTalks.html#Top%20Of%20Page
8. http://www.reikimaster.com.pk/reiki-history.ph

9. Brown, Fren, "Living Reiki, Takata's Teachings" no.2, 24-43;1992
10. http://www.reiki.org/FAQ/HistoryOfReiki.html
11. Ibid. Used by permission by William Lee Rand
12. Ibid. Used by permission by William Lee Rand
13. http://www.reiki.org/FAQ/HistoryOfReiki.html
14. http://www.practicalreiki.com/blog/tag/the-22-reiki-master-initiated-by-hawayo-takata/
15. Ibid.
16. Ellyard, Lawrence, *Reiki Healer- A Complete Guide to the Path and Practice of Reiki*, Lotus Press, Twin Lakes, Wisconsin 53181; 2004.
17. http://www.usuishikiryohoreiki.com/ogm/phyllis-paul/
18. Ibid.
19. https://reiki-conciliation.org/history/

Chapter Four

1. Ellyard, Lawrence, *Reiki Healer- A Complete Guide to the Path and Practice of Reiki*, Lotus Press, Twin Lakes, Wisconsin 53181, 2004.
2. http://www.reikipowerofgrace.com/assets/origins.html
3. Idid
4. Ellyard, Lawrence, *Reiki Healer- A Complete Guide to the Path and Practice of Reiki*, Lotus Press, Twin Lakes, Wisconsin 53181, 2004.
5. http://www.reikisystem.com
6. Ellyard, Lawrence, *Reiki Healer- A Complete Guide to the Path and Practice of Reiki*, Lotus Press, Twin Lakes, Wisconsin 53181, 2004.
7. http://www.usuishikiryohoreiki.com/ogm/phyllis-p
8. Ibid.
9. Maresca, Ingvarsson, Liliana, *La Nueva Historia del Kurama Yama Reiki*, 1ª. Edición, Editorial Distribuidora Lumen SRL, Buenos Aires, Argentina, Grupo Editorial Lumen México, D.F., México; 2003.
10. http://www.reiki.org/FAQ/MrsTakataTalks.html#Top%20Of%20Page

11. Ibid.
12. http://www.reiki.org/FAQ/HistoryOfReiki.html
13. "Reiki". Oxford English Dictionary (OED). 2003. Sino-Japanese readings were historically borrowed from Middle Chinese pronunciations reconstructed by Baxter-Sagart as lengkhj (靈氣).
14. Halpern, Jack (1993) [1990]. New Japanese-English Character Dictionary (新漢英字典) (NTC reprint ed.).   Kenkyūsha.
15. https://en.wikipedia.org/wiki/Reiki
16. Maresca, Ingvarsson, Liliana, *La Nueva Historia del Kurama Yama Reiki*, 1ª. Edición, Editorial Distribuidora Lumen SRL, Buenos Aires, Argentina, Grupo Editorial Lumen México, D.F., México; 2003.
17. https://en.wikipedia.org/wiki/Pseudociencia
18. https://scincebasedmedicine.org/reiki-fraudulent-misrepresentation/
19. *Lee, MS; Pittler, MH;* Ernst, E *(2008). "Effects of reiki in clinical practice: A systematic review of randomized clinical trials". International Journal of Clinical Practice (Systematic Review). 62 (6): 947–54.* doi:10.1111/j.1742- 1241. 2008.01729.x. PMID 18410352. In conclusion, the evidence is insufficient to suggest that reiki is an effective treatment for any condition. *Therefore,* the value of reiki remains unproven.
20. Reiki: Fraudulent Misrepresentation « Science-Based Medicine: Reiki: Fraudulent Misrepresentation « Science-Based Medicine, access date: May 28, 2016
21. Russell J, Rovere A, eds. *(2009).* "Reiki". American Cancer Society Complete Guide to Complementary and Alternative Cancer Therapies (2nd ed.). American Cancer Society. pp. *243–45.* ISBN 9780944235713.
22. "Reiki". Cancer Research UK. Archived from the original on 18 March 2015.
23. "Reiki: What You Need to Know". National Center for Complementary and Integrative Health Archived from the original on 11 April 2015
24. https://en.wikipedia.org/wiki/Alternative_medicine
25. https://www.merriam-webster.com/dictionary/medicine

26. Barnett, Libby, Chambers, Maggie, Davidson Susan, *Reiki, Energy Medicine*-Bringing Healing Touch into Home, Hospital, and Hospice, Healing Arts Press, Inner Traditions International, Rochester, Vermont; 1966.
27. Ibid.
28. Ibid.
29. Ibid.
30. https://www.englewoodhealth.org/service/graf-center-for-integrative-medicine
31. https://www.emersonwellness.org/
32. https://das.nh.gov/wellness/
33. https://en.wikipedia.org/wiki/Alternative_medicine
34. http://www.nbcnews.com/id/31190909/#.WhJ0SHaQyic
35. https://en.wikipedia.org/wiki/Electromagnetism
36. https://en.wikipedia.org/wiki/Moxibustion
37. Johnson, Jerry, Alan, PhD., D.T.C.M. (China), *The Secret Teachings of Energetic Medicine,* Vol.1, "Energetic Anatomy and Physiology," Pp: 29-31; The International Institute of Medical Qigong Publishing House, 2014.
38. https://www.schoolofhealth.com/medical-sciences/what-is-medical-science/
39. http://www./7senses.org.au/what-are-the-7-senses/
40. https://en.wikipedia.org/wiki/Qigong
41. https://energyhealingscience.com/soeh-2plc2/
42. https://www.sciencedirect.com/science/article/pii/S2005290113002082
43. https://www.youtube.com/watch?v=LS3wMC2BpxU
44. https://www.peterrussell.com/SCG/ideal.php
45. Ibid.
46. https://www.livescience.com/38234-is-reality-real-or-not.html
47. https://en.wikipedia.org/wiki/Alternative_medicine
48. Pert, Candice, B., PhD., Molecules of Emotion, Simon and Schuster, Inc., 1997
49. https://en.wikipedia.org/wiki/Metaphysics
50. Qian, Rene, Hands-On Brain- Rewiring the Brain Connections with the Position of the Hands Over the Head Technique, Blue Orbit Publications, ISBN: 978-1-7354096-3-4;2020
51. https://www.cancer.gov/about-cancer/treatment/cam

52. https://en.wikipedia.org/wiki/Vagus_nerv
53. https://www.frontiersin.org/articles/10.3389/fimmu.2017.0145 2/full
54. https://www.apa.org/helpcenter/stress/effects-nervous
55. Qian, Rene, The M.S.C.P. Principle, Page Publishing, Inc., N.Y., 2017
56. https://en.wikipedia.org/wiki/Alternative_medicine

Chapter Five

1. Churchland, Patricia, S., *Touching a Nerve, the self as Brain,* W.W. Norton and Company, Ney York, London First edition, 2013.
2. Ibid.
3. Tortora, Gerard J., Derrickson, Bryan, "Principles of Anatomy and Physiology", no. 4, 426-448, (2009).
4. Ibid.
5. https://en.wikipedia.org/wiki/History_of_anatomy
6. Ibid.
7. Ibid.
8. http://www.scielo.org.mx/scielo.php?script=sci_arttext&pid=S 0016-38132005000300012
9. https://www.ncbi.nlm.nih.gov/books/NBK546486/
10. https://behavior.org/wp-content/uploads/2019/04/BPv46-5-CHRISTOFIDOU.pdf
11. https://www.tandfonline.com/doi/abs/10.1080/0951508070142 2041
12. Pert, Candice, B., PhD., *Molecules of Emotion,* pp. 18-19.
13. Ibid.
14. Ibid.
15. www.neurogistics.com/the-science/what-are-neurotransmitters
16. Pert, Candice, B., PhD., *Molecules of Emotion,* p. 19-25
17. Ibid.
18. Pert, Candice, B., PhD., *Molecules of Emotion,* Simon and Schuster, Inc., 1997.
19. Pert, Candice, B., PhD., *Molecules of Emotion,* p. 70-72.
20. Pert, Candice, B., PhD., *Molecules of Emotion,* p. 126
21. Pert, Candice, B., PhD., *Molecules of Emotion,* pp. 70-72

22. Ibid.
23. Barnett, Libby, Chambers, Maggie, Davidson Susan, *Reiki, Energy Medicine-* Healing Touch into Home, Hospital, and Hospice, p 14, Healing Arts Press, Inner Traditions International, Rochester, Vermont; 1966.
24. https://link.springer.com/chapter/10.1007/978-94-011-9602-4_1?no-access=true
25. https://www.thefreedictionary.com/heaven
26. Ibid.
27. Citation by the author
28. https://en.wikipedia.org/wiki/Representation_(arts)
29. Citation by the author
30. https://en.wikipedia.org/wiki/Representation_(arts)
31. Barnett, Libby, Chambers, Maggie, Davidson Susan, *Reiki, Energy Medicine-* Healing Touch into Home, Hospital, and Hospice, p 14, Healing Arts Press, Inner Traditions International, Rochester, Vermont; 1966.
32. Pert, Candice, B., PhD., *Molecules of Emotion,* pp. 70-72
33. http://www.kathleenmilner.com/tera_mai_symbols.html

Chapter Six

1. Wolynn, Mark, *It Didn't Start with You*, How Inherent Family Trauma Shapes Who We Are and How to End the Cycle, Pp.76-77, Penguin Books, New York, New York 10014, 2017.
2. http://wiki.p2pfoundation.net/Embodied_Perception
3. www.groupofforty.com
4. www.Astro-Oracle.com
5. https://www.history.com/news/what-are-the-crystal-skulls
6. Morton, Cris, and, Thomas, Ceri, Louise, *The Mystery of the Crystal Skulls*, Bear & Company, Rochester, Vermont, pp.15-16, 2002.
7. https://allthatsinteresting.com/crystal-skull
8. https://www.history.com/news/what-are-the-crystal-skulls
9. https://en.wikipedia.org/wiki/Tzompantli
10. https://en.wikipedia.org/wiki/Kali
11. https://en.wikipedia.org/wiki/Capela_dos_Ossos

12. https://en.wikipedia.org/wiki/Capuchin_Cryp
13. https://www.huffpost.com/entry/7-things-to-know-about-la_b_8385476
14. https://www.scribd.com/doc/44528763/Mictecacihuatl-Santa-Muerte
15. https://www.google.com/search?q=huitzilopochtli&oq=Huitzil opochtli&aqs=chrome.0.0l8.5392j0j7&sourceid=c hrome&ie=UTF-8
16. https://en.wikipedia.org/wiki/Human_sacrifice_in_Aztec_cultu re
17. https://en.wikipedia.org/wiki/Human_sacrifice_in_Maya_cultu re
18. https://en.wikipedia.org/wiki/Sacred_Heart
19. https://en.wikipedia.org/wiki/Mesoamerican_religion
20. https://en.wikipedia.org/wiki/Noumenon

BIBLIOGRAPHY

Arun, P. (2006). Electronics. Alpha Sciences International Ltd. pp. 73–77. ISBN 1842652176

Bartlett, Sarah, The Secrets of the Universe in *100 Symbols*, Fair Winds Press, 2015 Quintessence Editions Ltd.

Biel, Andrew, "Trail Guide to the Body", third edition, p.17, 2005.

Brown, Fren, "Living Reiki, Takata's Teachings".1992

Browne, Sylvia. Harrison, Lyndsay, *The Truth About Psychics*. New Yor, New York.: Fireside, a division of Somon & Shuster, Inc., 2009.

Churchland, Patricia, S., *Touching a Nerve, the self as Brain,* W.W. Norton and Company, Ney York, London, First edition, 2013.

C. Polk and E. Postow, Handbook of Biological Effects of Electromagnetic Fields. Boca Raton, FL: CRC, 1986, P. 503

D. H. Fender, "Models of the human brain and the surrounding media: Their influence on the reliability of source localization," J. Clin. Neurophysiology., vol. 8, pp. 381–390,1991.

E. B. Lyskov, J. Juutilainen, V. Jousmaki, J. Partanen, S. Medvedev, and O. Hanninen,

"Effects of 45-Hz magnetic fields on the functional state of the human brain," Bioelectromagn, vol. 14, pp. 87–95, 1993.

Ellyard, Lawrence, *Reiki Healer- A Complete Guide to the Path and Practice of Reiki*, Lotus Press, Twin Lakes, Wisconsin 53181, 2004.

Enciclopedia Cultural, -Compton's Pictured Enciclopedia,- UTHEA Segunda Edición en español, 1957,1963, México, D.F.

Francis S, Rolls ET, Bowtell R, McGlone F, O'Doherty J, Browning A, Clare S, Smith E., Neuroreport, *The representation of pleasant touch in the brain and its relationship with taste and olfactory areas.* 1999 Feb 25; 10(3):453-9.

Hudman, Andy, "Learning and Memory", no.1, 1-11, (2006)

H. Zhou and A. van Oosterom, "Computation of the potential distribution in a four-layer anisotropic concentric spherical volume conductor,"IEEE Trans. Biomed. Eng., vol. 39, pp. 154–158, 1992.

Jhonson, Jerry, Alan, PhD., D.T.C.M. (China), *The Secret Teachings of Energetic Medicine,* Vol.1, "Energetic Anatomy and Physilogy," Pp: 29-31; The International Institute of Medical Qigong Publishing House, 2014.

Johansson RS J Physiol. *Tactile sensibility in the human hand: receptive field characteristics of mechanoreceptive units in the glabrous skin area.* 1978 Aug; 28;101-25.

Johnson KO Curr Opin Neurobiol. *The roles and functions of cutaneous mechanoreceptors* 2001 Aug; 11(4):455-61.

Lindemann, Mary, Medicine, and Society in Early Modern Europe (2nd ed.). Cambridge, United Kingdom: Cambridge University Press. 2010

Löken LS, Wessberg J, Morrison I, McGlone F, Olausson H., *Coding of pleasant touch by unmyelinated afferents in humans.* Nat. Neurosci. 2009 May; 12(5):547-8.

Lu, Henry C. *Chinese System of Foods for Health & Healing.* New York.: Sterling Publishing Co., Inc., 2000.

Marsh, Clint, *"The Mentalist's Handbook"*, *An explorer's Guide to Astral, Spirit, and Psychic Worlds*, Red Wheel/Weiser Books, San Francisco, CA/Newburyport,MA; First published 2008.

Meske, Doug, MSW, Ph.D., "Our Six Emotional Needs", 8th. Edition, Wisconsin, 1988

Nardo, Don, *The Salem with Trials-American History-*, Lucent Books, Thompson Gale, Farmington Hills, MI., 2007.

Nordin M J Physiol. *Low-threshold mechanoreceptive and nociceptive units with unmyelinated (C) fibers in the human supraorbital nerve.* 1990 Jul; 426():229-40. *Cutaneous afferents provide information about knee joint movements in humans.* Edin B J Physiol. 2001 Feb 15; 531(Pt 1):289-97.

Pagels, Elaine, *The Gnostic Gospels*, Vintage Books, a Division of Random House, Inc., New York, 1989.

Pert, Candice, B., PhD., *Molecules of Emotion,* Simon and Schuster, Inc., 1997.

Qian, Rene. *The M.S.C.P. Principle.* New York: Page Publishing; First Published, 2017.

Roig, Olga, *Símbolos Ocultos y Mágicos*, EDIMAT libros, S.A., Madrid, España,

R. S. Hosek, A. Sances, Jr., R. W. Jodat, and S. J. Larson, "The contributions of intracerebral currents to the EEG and evoked potentials" IEEE Trans. Biomed. Eng., vol. BME-25, pp. 405–413, 1978.

Usui, Mikao, Dr., Arjava, Petter, Frank, The Original Reiki Handbook of Dr. Mikao Usui, Lotus Press, Shangri-La, Twin Lakes, WI.,4th. Eng., Ed., 2003.

Vallbo AB, Johansson RS Hum Neurobiol. *Properties of cutaneous mechanoreceptors in the human hand related to touch sensation.*1984; 3(1):3-14.

Vallbo A, Olausson H, Wessberg J, Norrsell U Brain Res. *A system of unmyelinated afferents for innocuous mechanoreception in the human skin.*1993 Nov 19; 628(1-2):301-4.

Vernon, Roberta, In Focus *Palmistry*,Your Personal Guide, Wellfleet Press, NewYork,N.Y., 2018.

Weinstein S. (1968). "Intensive, extensive aspects of tactile sensitivity as a function of body part, sex and laterality," in The Skin Senses, ed Kenshalo D., editor. (Springfield, IL: Charles C. Thomas), 195–222.

Wolynn, Mark, *It Didn't Start with You*, How Inherent Family Trauma Shapes Who We Are and How to End the Cycle, Pp.76-77, Penguin Books, New York, New York 10014, 2017.

www.ingramcontent.com/pod-product-compliance
Lightning Source LLC
Chambersburg PA
CBHW060055100426
42742CB00014B/2839